Planetary Powers

The Morin Method

Patti Tobin Brittain

ISBN-10: 0-86690-616-9
ISBN-13: 978-0-86690-616-6

Cover Design: Jack Cipolla

Published by:
American Federation of Astrologers, Inc.
6535 S. Rural Road
Tempe, AZ 85283

www.astrologers.com

Printed in the United States of America

Dedication

To Gerhard Howling, my instructor, who showed us the truth by example
and guided us with his light.

To James H. Holden and Bette Ford Starr, I extend my deepest gratitude
for your tenacity and making this publication possible . . . again!

Contents

Section III

Section IV

Preface to the Second Edition

This reprint of Patti Tobin Brittain's landmark textbook on the Morin Method was suggested by James Herschel Holden, who supplied images of the pages from his personal copy of the first edition.

Kris Brandt Riske re-formatted the pages, and Bette Ford Starr edited the text with the cooperation of the author. Mrs. Brittain, Mrs. Starr, and Mr. Holden were students of the late Gerhard Angel Houwing (1923-2009), master expositor of the Morin Method of Horoscope Interpretation.

This book provides a course in the Morin Method following the teaching procedure used by Mr. Houwing in his classes.

Foreword to the First Edition

This book has one purpose: to help the astrologer form an accurate judgment of a given planet in a nativity and then define the events, circumstances, and experiences the native will encounter during his or her lifetime.

John-Baptiste Morin formulated a concise and concrete method of synthesis that enables the astrologer to determine the quality of action of a planet as a producer of good or evil. With this knowledge the astrologer can more effectively assist clients, helping them to avert future unpleasant events and direct them in the departments that bring happiness and fulfillment.

Having searched for this knowdedge and finding none that withstood prolonged observation to my satisfaction, I started a study of Morin's teachings. No books were available in this country, nor had any been translated to English at that time. My instructor, who introduced me to the renowned work of Morin, studied in Europe for many years and had applied this systematic approach in his astrological work and research. He was instrumental in the translation of Morin's *Astrologia Gallica*, which was made available in this country in 1972.

The teachings of Morin under the guidance of this profound scholar has been so valuable to me that I want to share it with others who might be searching. A small group of astrologers studied with this brilliant man for many years. He gave enormously of himself and his wealth of knowledge, his only purpose being to help us become better astrologers. Confident and forceful, he had an immense force of mind and spirit. He demanded the concise, the specific, the concrete; he scorned the vague, the confused, the irresolute. He felt it was worse to be irresolute than to be wrong. "Be specific," he would snap in the form of a sharp command. "Leave the vague and confused to the philosophers, he would demand, constantly urging us to be accurate in our astrological judgments. What amazed us all was his accuracy and precision when interpreting a chart he knew nothing about, never hedging or back-tracking. This teacher, an incontestably superior astrologer, was a master of the teachings of Morin.

Planetary Powers does not pretend to survey the entire field of Morin's theories. Rather, it proposes to give the basic rules and principles and concentrate on the fundamentals. Each basic principle is followed by an explanation and examples. I have attempted to cut down any vast tangle of rhetoric in favor of being specific. Some statements may sound fatalistic as it is impossible to guard against expressions that may have this implication. With brevity in mind, I have attempted to express a few essential factors of a whole series. Unless these modifications are borne constantly in mind, it will be impossible to successfully use them.

Morin formulated a comprehensive and judicious method of synthesis. His Theory of Determinations enables one to judge how a planet will act in a given horoscope and if it will be a producer of benefits or adversities. Properly applied, Morin's teachings will resolve some of the most complicated problems in the art of synthesis and in forming accurate judgments. It is to aid in this most desirable achievement that the writing of this book is undertaken.

All horoscopes in this book are calculated using the Tropical System with Placidus house cusps.

Patti Tobin
July 1980

Foreword to the Second Edition

Jean-Baptiste Morin, 1583-1656

Morin was a medical doctor, astronomer, mathematician, and astrologer. He had an extensive practice among the notables of Paris. And he gave astrological advice to Cardinal Richelieu, who didn't like him personally, but respected his astrological judgment. Morin was even called to be present at the birth of the infant who became Louis XIV, so that he could cast a precise horoscope for him. He was without a doubt France's greatest astrologer.

My personal instructor was the late Gerhard Houwing, who was probably the most brilliant man I ever met. He was working and living in Europe in the early 1950s, when he came across a copy of Morin's *Astrologia Gallica*. It had been translated into German, but he was fluent in several languages, including German. After a careful examination of the contents, he was thrilled that finally he had found an astrology book that made sense. After many years of searching, he had finally found the key to astrology, through Morin's work.

Gerhard was an engineer who had taken a position with a company in Dallas, Texas. He started to give astrology lessons in that city in 1970, and I was fortunate enough to be in those classes. In our class we never used any books or props. The class consisted of complete concentration in listening to our instructor.

We memorized the Morin rules given to us by Gerhard. He taught a systematic approach to reading a chart, and he constantly urged us to be concise, specific and accurate: "You must memorize, you must study, you must put in the time! And if you are willing to do this, you will learn to read a chart with accuracy. If these rules of the Morin Method are committed to memory, you can resolve some of the most complicated problems in the art of synthesis and form accurate judgments."

I wrote this book so that the reader can learn there is truth in astrology that can be obtained through Morin's method. This is a basic text with many examples to make it easier to understand.

Finally, to my instructor Gerhard Houwing, I dedicate this book with gratitude.

Patti Tobin Brittain
November 2010

Introduction

In modern times, astrologers are discovering through statistical scientific research that many of the principles expounded by the ancient astrologers are accurate. The treatises by William Lilly and Firmicus Maternus are among the ones being tested, but the astrologer whose principles have provided us with the most startling results is Morin de Villefranche, perhaps better known by the Latin name under which he wrote: Morinus.

Jean Baptiste Morin de Villefranche was born in 1583 and died in 1656. Well educated, he was a mathematician, physician, and astrologer. Cardinal Richelieu used his services as an astrologer for twenty years. His principle work was the twenty-six volume Astrologia Gallica.

Morinus set forth a precise method of synthesizing a horoscope that indicates how early or late in life events take place, as well as the intensity with which they occcur. Using the essential nature of signs, planets, and houses, one can accurately use his system to judge a person's character and mentality and, with reasonable acccuracy, judge the events of the person's life. I say "with reasonable accuracy" because astrology today is groping toward truth, and there are still many holes in specific astrological prediction. Perhaps there is no Ultimate Rule in astrology; the more we learn, the more we realize there is to learn. The total complexity of astrological prediction in terms of timing and specifics boggles the mind.

Patti Tobin, a serious and profound Scorpio, is well versed in the Morinus method. It has been said that the genius takes the complex and makes it simple. Patti has done this with the system of Morin de Villefranche in this book. It is an important contribution to the field of astrology. Those who study it and apply its method will be quality astrologers.

Susan Horton
July 11, 1980

What a glorious power is given to man, never to do any action which God
will not approve, and to welcome whatever God appoints for him.—Marcus Aurelius

Section I

Planetary Powers

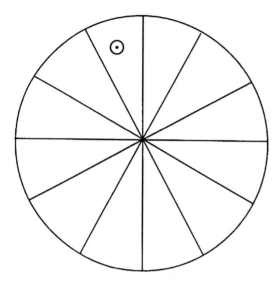

Success, fame, honors

1. A planet can realize the object of its determination.

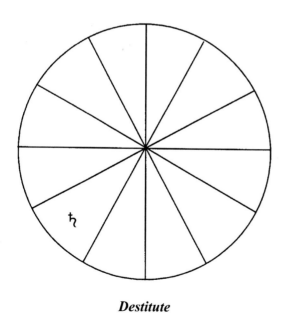

Destitute

2. A planet can prevent the object of its determination.

3. A planet will not only produce benefits but turn away harm. Give protection.

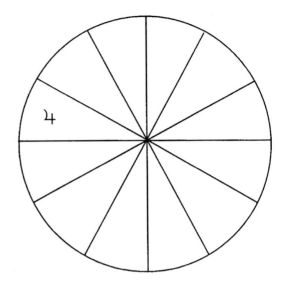

Victory over enemies

4. A planet can realize its objective and destroy it once realized.

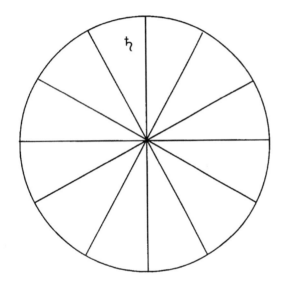

A rise to fame and downfall

5. A planet can be a source of misfortune (Mars in the eighth house) or fortune (Venus in the second house).

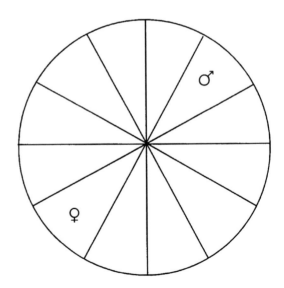

Fortune or Misfortune

Theory of Determinations

The planets are prognostic signs of things to come in the future—unless they are in some way prevented—but also a cause of them if they do take place. Before a horoscope can be utilized for predictive conclusions, the potential and the promise must be determined.

Morin's Theory of Determinations is the exact evaluation of a planet's action and its specific influence upon the person's life. Through his systematic approach, events and circumstances and their extent and nature can be defined, as well as with what measure of success or failure.

The horoscope taken as a whole does not cause a specific event or quality. Nor do the houses directly produce the affairs that are attributed to them; they only determine the influences of the planets and signs present therein.

The position or ruler of a planet in a house indicates a group of events or affairs may, or may not, happen to a person, but not the materilizaion of these matters. This realization, or the contrary, can only be determined by the *essential nature*, *analogy*, and *cosmic state* of the planet in question. The same elements determine the quality and quantity of the effects.

Consequently, the planets:

1. Relate to the kind of thing, event, or matter.

2. Indicate whether the event will be realized for the person.

3. Define the quality and extent of this realization.

4. Reveal the causes of their realization.

5. Reveal the causes of their obstruction.

6. Reveal the cause of their loss, once acquired.

7. They can cause the realization to *transform* itself into a source of happiness or disaster for the native.

Thus, the house meanings represent what could occur in the life of a person; the planets materialize the house meanings in a good or bad sense, according to the determinations. Morin established a precise method of analyzing these factors. Once the basics are mastered, his analytical and systematic approach will add a new dimension in chart interpretation.

Cosmic State and Local Determinations

Each planet acts through the sign it is in, and this action is influenced by the aspects formed with other planets. But the *essential nature* of the planet always prevails: Mars will always be Martian and the effect of Saturn will always be Saturnine. This effect, however, will be favored or hindered by other factors of the combination. The *essential nature* of the sign imparts certain qualities to that of the planet which acts through the sign. This combination of factors result in the Dignities and Debilities (cosmic state) of the planets.

Consequently, a planet's influence is strengthened when in its Dignity and weakened when in Debility. In addition, there are two varieties: Essential and Accidental. A planet in a sign in which it is strengthened is in one of its Essential Dignities, and in a house in which it is strengthened, in its Accidental Dignity.

Thus, through all the modifying factors of the *essential nature* of a planet in a given horoscope, we obtain its accidental nature. But the direction of its effect and particular influence on the native depends on other factors called Deteterminations.

Rules for Determining the *Cosmic State* of the Planets

1. Consider the essential nature of the planet and if it is benefic or malefic. And then its cosmic state according to:

2. The zodiacal sign (cosmic state) in which it is found. If not in its Domicile, examine its Disposer and determine the state of that planet.

3. By the relations with other planets by conjunction and aspect, examine the quality of these aspects.

4. The planets local Determination (Terrestrial State) by:

    a. House position.

    b. House rulership.

5. The character of the house, if it is benefic or malefic, and if the planet's essential nature has *analogy* with the house, or if the planet *acquires an analogy* with the house by sign or aspect.

In the determination of the *cosmic state*, the *essential nature* of the planet will always prevail, but the manifestation is reinforced or weakened by these other factors.

The Houses

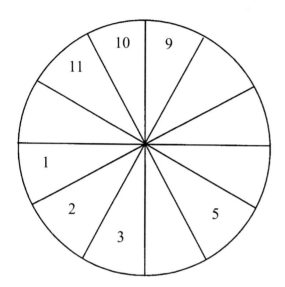

Benefic Houses

Benefic Houses

Beneific houses bring the events, matters, and experiences in life that one wants, i.e., good health, money, security, intellect, love, success, recognition, friends.

The benefic houses are: one, two, three, five, nine, ten, eleven.

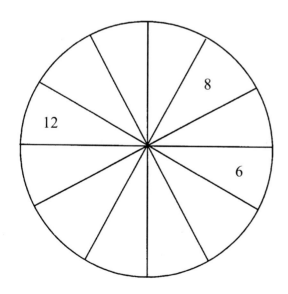

Malefic Houses

Malefic Houses

The malefic houses produce the matters and events in life that one does not want, i.e. , illness, surgery, accidents, poverty, confinement, sorrow, enemies, loss, death.

The malefic houses are: six, eight, twelve.

Partly Benefic, Partly Malefic Houses

Four and seven are partly benefic and malefic. The benefic part of house four is real estate, home, parents, inherited possessions and real estate; the malefic part is conditions surrounding the end of life. House seven is benefic in marriage, long-lasting love relations and all partnerships, malefic in the meanings of open enemies, war, fights, lawsuits, and confrontations.

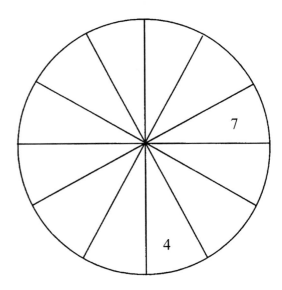

Partly Benefic, Partly Malefic Houses

The Signs

The signs are classified as benefic or malefic.

Benefic Sign	Ruler		Malefic Sign	Ruler
Taurus	Venus		Aries	Mars
Gemini	Mercury		Virgo	Mercury
Cancer	Moon		Scorpio	Mars
Leo	Sun		Capricorn	Saturn
Libra	Venus		Aquarius	Saturn and Uranus
Sagittarius	Jupiter		Pisces	Jupiter and Neptune

Benefic signs are ruled by benefic planets. Malefic signs are ruled by malefic planets. The exceptions are Virgo and Pisces. Virgo is the mundane ruler of a malefic house (house six); Pisces is the mundane ruler of the malefic house twelve.

Aquarius and Pisces have two rulers each. Uranus and Neptune were not known to Morin, as they had not been discovered at that time. For an accurate synthesis, both Saturn and Uranus must be assessed when judging Aquarius, and both Jupiter and Neptune when judging Pisces.

Division According to Gender

Gender of Signs

Masculine: Aries, Gemini, Leo, Libra, Sagittarius, Aquarius (uneven natural house numbers)

Feminine: Taurus, Cancer, Virgo, Scorpio, Capricorn, Pisces (even natural house numbers)

Gender of Planets

Masculine: Mars, Sun, Jupiter, Saturn

Feminine: Moon, Venus

Neutral: Mercury is considered neutral until it is in a sign; then its gender forms. (Mercury in Aries is like reading Mercury conjunct Mars; Mercury in Libra is like Mercury conjunct Venus.)

When a planet is in a sign of the same gender it is more agreeable and therefore more powerful. Example: With Jupiter in Sagittarius, planet and sign are the same gender (masculine). With Jupiter in Pisces, Jupiter is masculine and Pisces is feminine. When the planet and sign are of the same gender, the action will be more powerful.

Author's Note: Morin knew nothing of Uranus and Neptune as they had not yet been discovered. History has recorded the accuracy and success of his predictions.

The Planets

The planets are classified as benefic or malefic. Benefics tend to be constructive, and malefics tend to be destructive:

- Benefic planets: Sun, Moon, Venus, Jupiter
- Malefic planets: Mars, Saturn, Uranus
- Sometimes benefic, sometimes malefic: Neptune
- Neutral (depending on sign, position, aspects): Mercury
- Not included (not enough research for accurate conclusion): Pluto

The planets are divided according to their gender:

- Masculine planets: Sun, Mars, Jupiter, Saturn , Uranus
- Feminine planets: Moon, Venus, Neptune

Morin considered Mercury as masculine, but other authors classify it as androgynous, feminine when in contact with feminine planets, masculine when in contact with masculine planets.

Essential Dignities and Debilities of the Planets

Planet	Domicile	Detriment	Exaltation	Fall
☉	♌	♒	♈	♎
☽	♋	♑	♉	♏
☿	♊ ♍	♐ ♓	♍ ♒	♌ ♓
♀	♉ ♎	♏ ♈	♓	♍
♂	♈ ♏	♎ ♉	♑	♋
♃	♐ ♓	♊ ♍	♋	♑
♄	♑ ♒	♋ ♌	♎	♈
♅	♒	♌	♏	♉
♆	♓	♍	♌	♒
♇	♏	♉		

Triplicity

According to Morin, the rulers of triplicity are those planets that have their domicile in one of the signs composing the triplicity. Planets in triplicity are:

- Sun in Sagittarius
- Moon in Pisces
- Mercury in Libra, Taurus, Capricorn
- Venus in Capricorn, Gemini, Aquarius
- Mars in Leo, Sagittarius, Pisces
- Jupiter in Aries, Leo
- Saturn in Taurus, Virgo, Gemini
- Uranus in Gemini, Libra
- Neptune in Cancer, Scorpio

Peregrine (planets in signs other than above)

- Sun in Taurus, Gemini, Cancer, Virgo, Scorpio, Capricorn, Pisces
- Moon in Aries, Gemini, Leo, Virgo, Libra, Sagittarius, Aquarius
- Mercury in Aries, Cancer, Scorpio
- Venus in Cancer, Leo, Sagittarius
- Mars in Gemini, Virgo, Aquarius
- Jupiter in Taurus, Libra, Aquarius
- Saturn in Scorpio, Sagittarius, Pisces

Planets in Domicile: When a planet is in its own sign, it is pure and intense. Its effect is constant. The planet will function at its highest level. It signifies the permanence or stability of the things the house promises. It is even more effective when the planet and sign are the same gender.

Planets in Exaltation: An exalted planet has an increase in force. Exalted planets attract benefits, which come in spurts throughout life. Planets in exaltation do not increase quality but do increase quantity. The nature of the planet determines the character of its effect. The nature and cosmic state of its disposer, house position, and aspects must be examined.

Planets in Detriment (Exile): A planet cannot operate freely in detriment because it is in a sign whose nature is contrary to its own. Its effect is hindered and obscured. A planet in detriment (exile) is obstructed due to the alteration of its essential nature. It's even worse if the planet and sign are different genders. A planet in exile will always act first according to its own nature, and then according to the nature of its disposer.

Planets in Fall: When a planet is in a sign opposite its exaltation, it loses its strength and the character of its force because it is in a sign that is at cross purposes with its own nature. It's a conflict of purpose between sign and planet. Judge the planet's nature and the nature of its sign. Its disposer must be examined carefully as it can add to the problem or help it. The disposer's nature and cosmic state will help with the final judgment.

Planets in Triplicity: Planets in triplicity give limited abilities, but are remarkable in certain directions. The native seems to get breaks through other people. Always check its disposer, asking whether it is a malefic or benefic and whether it is in good *cosmic state*. This could be a help or a hindrance.

Planets in Peregrine: Check the nature of the planet and its cosmic state. Are the planet and sign harmonious? Does the planet or sign have analogy with the house? Or is either one antagonistic with its house meaning? If the genders (sign and planet) agree, it will be more constructive; if they disagree, it will be less constructive. Look to the disposer and analyze its cosmic state.

The planet's *analogy* with the house *and cosmic state of the sign are the first judgments you should identify*. The above has a great influence on the quality and force of the planet.

Examples of Friendships and Enemies Among the Planets

Agreement and Accord: Sun and Jupiter have analogy with success and life; Jupiter and Venus with regard to luck, wealth, and friends; and Moon and Venus with love and marriage. There is friendship between two planets whose domiciles are in mutually favorable aspect, such as Sun and Mars (Leo and Aries), and Jupiter and Moon (Pisces and Cancer). Additionally, malefic and benefic planets can be friends. Saturn and Jupiter cooperate because this favors the capacity for knowledge as well as having analogy for financial gain and keeping money safe. Saturn and Mercury cooperate because this favors intellectual depth and a profound mind combined with discrimination. Mercury and Mars (this needs careful observation) give an alert, active, and inquisitive mind along with vivacity of the intellect.

Hostile and Antagonistic: We have established that a malefic and a benefic can be friendly and can do good things in a chart. However, if by determination the malefic overpowers the benefic, the results can be: Mars and Mercury causing intellectual audacity; Sun and Mars causing arrogance;

Moon and Mercury causing gossip, indiscretion, or rashness; or Mars and Venus causing the need for peace and love after inciting fights and disputes. Saturn and Sun can gain success, presitge, and honors, only to be undermined, leading to loss (unless Saturn acquires help, with a good aspect to Jupiter or another benefic). And lastly, Saturn and Mars, as this provokes dangers and difficulties, and can be a threat to life.

Determining Natural Analogy

Natural analogy between the nature of the planet and the house meanings should be carefully analyzed. Certain planets have an agreement, likeness or some other correspondence between their nature and the house meaning. There is a partial similarity or affinity in certain circumstances or concerns on which a comparison may be based.

When this analogy exists, the promises of that house will materialize. The more the planet is assisted in its cosmic state, the more it is likely to produce good; the more it is impaired, the more it will produce difficulties.

Before a determination can be made, the planet's affinity by analogy must be judged. As an example, the Sun in house ten indicates honors as the Sun has natural analogy with honors. But the Sun in this house could accidentally deny honors if in detriment or fall, or receiving bad aspects from the malefics. Or, any honors received would be attended by difficulties and frustrations. However, due to the analogy of the Sun with honors and the meaning of the tenth house, the materialization of these matters could be expected.

In addition, Mars in the seventh provokes fights and open enemies as the essential nature of Mars has analogy with these matters. Jupiter in the second brings wealth as its essential nature has analogy with money and abundance. Saturn in the sixth or twelfth can provoke a chronic illness as its nature bears analogy with ill health. Saturn by nature denies any honors in house ten, but could bring them accidentally if in its own sign or in exaltation and trine the benefics. But these honors would materialize through effort and stress; yet once achieved, they may not bring total satisfaction.

Therefore, one must always consider the essential nature of the planet in question, its analogy or antagonism with the house in question, and then the other detertminations.

A planet that has analogy with a house brings the circumstances, people, and events of that house:

1. In quantity (i.e., no money or great wealth)
2. In intensity (i.e., light, medium, deep)
3. In speed of results (early or late in life)
4. In duration (fleeting or permanent, forever, a year)

Acquired Analogy

Benefic planets have *analogy* with benefic houses. Malefic planets have *analogy* with malefic houses. This is called natural analogy. *Analogy* may occur, however, by ways other than planetary house position. This is called acquired analogy.

A planet *acquires analogy*:

- By sign
- By dispositor
- By aspect
- By house

Acquired Analogy by Sign

A planet will *acquire analogy* by sign if the planet occupies a sign which has analogy with the house.

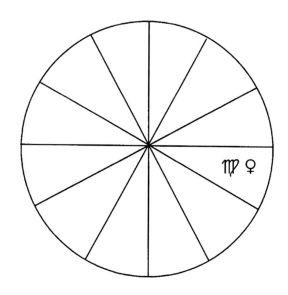

Acquired Analogy by Sign

Venus in Virgo in house six:

1. The essential nature of house six is malefic.

2. The essential nature of Venus is benefic.

3. The essential nature of Venus, a benefic, has no analogy with the malefic nature of the sixth house of health.

4. Venus is in the sign of Virgo and therefore acquires analogy with the sixth house by sign.

The benefic Venus, in itself, has no analogy with the house of health and would protect over any illness and give very few. By acquiring analogy through the sign of Virgo, the native would have many health problems, starting early in life and lasting throughout life. The native would always recover and the illnesses would not be disabling. Venus is in its fall.

Saturn in Taurus in house two:

1. The essential nature of house two is benefic.

2. The essential nature of Saturn is malefic.

3. The essential nature of Saturn, a malefic, has no analogy with the benefic meaning of house two—money.

4. However, Saturn is in the sign of Taurus and acquires analogy by sign.

The native will obtain wealth, but it may not be enough to suit him, or his frugal habits may interfere with his ability to enjoy the money.

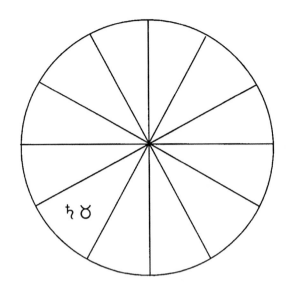

Acquired Analogy by Sign

Acquired Analogy by Sign

Jupiter in Scorpio in house twelve:

1. The essential nature of house twelve is malefic.

2. The essential nature of Jupiter is benefic.

3. The essential nature of Jupiter has no analogy with the nature of the malefic house twelve.

4. However, Jupiter is in Scorpio, and therefore acquires analogy with the meanings of house twelve.

Much would depend on the dispositor's cosmic state and house position of Mars. If in good cosmic state, the adverse meanings of house twelve will be somewhat lessened, but if in bad cosmic state, the effect will be worse.

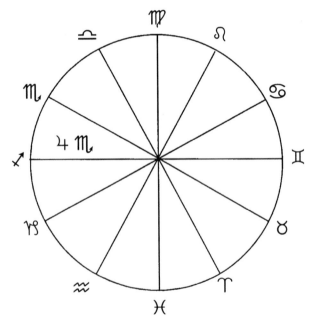

Acquired Analogy by Sign

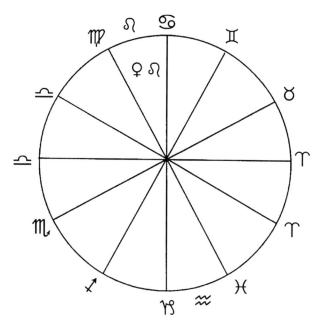

Venus in Leo in house ten:

1. The essential nature of house ten is benefic.

2. The essential nature of Venus is benefic.

3. The essential nature of Venus has no analogy with the meanings of fame, but does have analogy with good social position.

4. Venus in Leo acquires analogy by sign because Leo has analogy with fame. The cosmic state of the dispositor will dictate the promises of tenth house matters.

Acquired Analogy by Sign

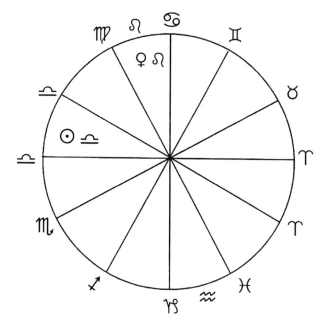

Venus in Leo in house ten is disposed by the Sun in Libra in house twelve:

1. The dispositor of Venus is in fall.

2. It is posited in the malefic house twelve.

3. The native will achieve honors and have success and happiness at the beginning, but his ventures could easily turn into failure or sadness. (This configuration is from the horoscope of former President Jimmy Carter).

A planet, acts with great power and according to its nature when it occupies a house which is in harmony or has an affinity with its natural analogies. When a planet is located in a house whose meanings do not correspond to its analogies, it hinders or destroys the things that house signifies.

Acquired Analogy by Dispositor

17

Acquired Analogy by Aspect

Jupiter in Cancer in house eight:

1. The essential nature of Jupiter is benefic.

2. Jupiter is posited in the malefic house eight.

3. Jupiter has no analogy with accidents or surgery and close calls with death.

4. However, Jupiter receives a square from Mars, a malefic planet in its detriment. Jupiter now acquires analogy with the adverse meanings of the eighth house.

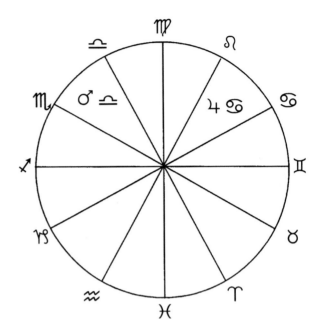

Acquired Analogy by Aspect

Venus in Libra in house six:

1. The essential nature of house six is malefic—illness.

2. The essential nature of Venus is benefic.

3. Venus has no analogy with disease and illness. It is in its domicile.

4. However, Venus recieves an opposition from the malefic Saturn in its fall from the malefic house twelve.

5. Venus now acquires analogy with the malefic meanings of house six.

6. Venus in domicile is opposition Saturn in fall, indicating a pattern of long periods of serious health problems followed by periods of good health.

In determining the degree of benefit or adversity that the planet sending the aspect will have, it is necessary to observe:

1. The nature of the planet sending the aspect—benefic or malefic.

2. If the planet is located in a benefic or malefic house.

3. The nature and state of its depositor.

4. The type of aspect it is sending.

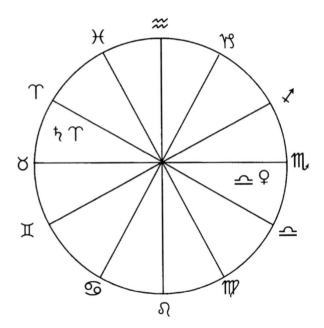

Acquired Analogy by Aspect

18

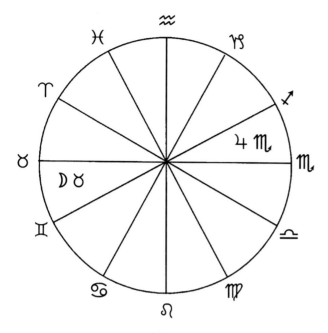

Moon in Taurus in house one:

1. The Moon in Taurus in house one is exalted and therefore in good cosmic state.

2. The Moon receives an opposition from Jupiter, the ruler of house eight.

3. Jupiter is in Scorpio, the natural ruler of house eight.

4. The malefic significations of house eight are transmitted to the first house of life.

Acquired Analogy by Aspect

Acquired Analogy by House

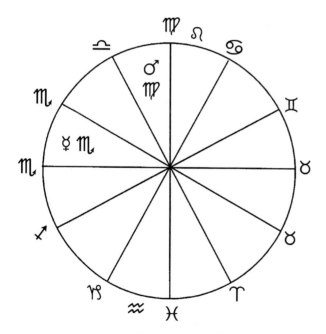

Mercury in Scorpio in house twelve:

1. Mercury in house twelve, ruler of house eight and ten.

2. Mercury is disposed by Mars, ruler of house twelve and posited in house ten.

3. Mars rules the Ascendant, the house of life (in the sign of Virgo).

4. The high position of the native caused many enemies. The native's profession brought danger to his life. The native's profession and the danger to his life caused him to go into exile.

5. The meanings of house ten and eight are transmitted to the house of confinement.

Acquired Analogy by House

Every planet whose nature has some analogy to the meanings of the house it occupies, or rules over, grants that, whether good or adverse, will come to pass in some way. If the planet's nature is contrary to the meanings of the house, that planet will remove, impede, limit, or deny the matters of the house.

Analogy of the Planets with the Houses

The planets and houses have many meanings too numerous to list here. This list, however, should convey the basic principle of analogy.

House One: Personality, mentality, appearance, general state of health, temperament, morals. The Ascendant is considered to be a compendium of the twelve houses. It is the house of physical life. The Sun, Moon, Mercury, and Jupiter have analogy with house one.

House Two: money, wealth, and lifeless or mobile possessions. Jupiter and Venus have analogy. Mars has no analogy; it makes a lot, spends a lot. The Sun has no analogy as money comes in but goes out just as quickly. Saturn has no analogy with wealth, or if it comes, he may not enjoy it, or it is never the amount he desires. Saturn in Capricorn, Aquarius, Libra, or Scorpio: money is difficult to obtain, but long-lasting.

House Three: Mentality, relatives (brothers, sisters, cousins), communication, short trips. The concrete mind. Mercury and Saturn have an analogy with the mind; Saturn has analogy with reasoning power. The Moon, Sun, and Neptune have analogy with emotions. The Moon, Mercury, and Mars have analogy with travel. Mercury has analogy with relatives.

House Four: Parents, real estate, inheritance, the home, carries the basic concept "hereditary mass," conditions surrouuding the end of life. Jupiter, Venus, the Sun, and Moon have analogy with parents. Saturn has analogy with real estate, as well as conditions surrounding the end of life.

House Five: The sensual life, sex, love affairs, children, pregnancy, sports, investments, games of chance, amusements. Venus has analogy with love. Mars and the Sun have analogy with passion and the sex act. Mars and Jupiter have analogy with sports and speculation. Moon, Jupiter, and Venus have analogy with the quantity of children. No analogy with fertility: Sun, Saturn, Mars. No analogy with great passion: Saturn.

House Six: Illness, obligations, work, servants, hygiene, personal work or service, domestic animals, comfort. Venus, Jupiter, and Mercury have analogy with servants. Saturn, Mars, Uranus, and Neptune have analogy with illness. The Moon in this house will give a lot of trouble of a small nature, but it will not provoke, produce, or prevent disease. This house also rules people paid for a service—physician, employee, dentist, cleaning personnel, etc.

House Seven: Unions, lasting love, marriage, partnerships, open enemies, fights, lawsuits, contracts. Venus and Jupiter have analogy with marriage. Mars, Saturn, and Uranus have analogy with open enemies. The Moon has analogy with the public. The Moon has no analogy with marriage.

House Eight: Death, accidents, and close calls with death, surgery, inheritance. The eighth house carries the basic concept of "deterioration." It is not the house of passion and sex, which is to be judged from house five! House eight is associated with disease and surgical procedures of the sex organs. Mars, Saturn, Uranus, and Neptune have analogy with a violent or painful death. Venus, Jupiter, and the Moon have analogy with inheritance and gifts of money, especially the Moon in Cancer or Taurus.

House Nine: The mind and mentality (together with houses one and three), higher education, the ability to deal in abstract concepts, knowledge outside of everyday matters, religion, long journeys, foreign matters, law, and spirituality. Mercury, Jupiter, and Saturn, have analogy with the mind. Mars, Moon, Mercury, and Jupiter have analogy with travel. Mercury and Saturn have analogy with studies.

House Ten: Honors, prestige, fame, reputation, and authority, and rise in social rank, the profession, career, and boss. The Sun, Moon, and Jupiter have analogy with honors and prestige. Venus has analogy with a good social postion and success. Saturn has no analogy with fame and honors. Saturn in house ten will gain success, but have many ups and downs—or a complete downfall.

House Eleven: Friends, protectors, promoters, supporters, advisors, social life, clubs, and organizations. Jupiter, Venus, the Moon, and the Sun have analogy with friends, protectors, and promoters.

House Twelve: Trials, obstacles, sorrows, confinement, hospitals, institutions, secret enemies, illness, misfortune, all the backhanded thrusts of life, calumny, misery, isolation, neglect, loss, (including honor!), persecution, convents, rectories, and religious orders. Saturn, Mars, Uranus, and Neptune have analogy with most twelfth house matters, and with good planets gives peace and contentment in solitude.

Principal Significations and Analogies of the Planets

Moon: Mother, wife, daughters, widows, travelers, the public, numerous children, changes and uncertainty, public places.

Sun: Father, husband, all those invested with honor (kings, governors, etc.), high rank, fame, powerful friends.

Mercury: Younger brothers, servants, orators, writers, poets, secretaries, merchants, thieves, forgers, contracts, transactions.

Venus: wife, mother, sisters, daughters, mistresses, artists, madams, female beggars, rewards, profit and success, lucky love affairs.

Mars: Husband, older brothers, open enemies, military people, doctors, lawyers, robbers, victory, triumph, duels, ambush, theft, murderers, rapists, adulterers, dissipation, prisons.

Jupiter: Diplomats, government employees, mayors , church dignitaries, advisors, coaches, wealth, rewards, fame, profit, freedom.

Saturn: Ancestors, grandfather, father, servants, old people, theologians, farmers, monks, hermits, beggars, hang-men, high office, secret enemies, infamy, exile, social downfall, failure.

Uranus, Neptune, and Pluto were not known to Morin, yet his predictions were of such precision that for twenty years he was an influential voice in the affairs of state. In an effort to present his true teachings and remain truthful to his theory of determinations, these planets have been omitted.

"He who is knowing can avert many of
the stars' effects by understanding their
nature and preparing himself ahead of time."—Ptolemy

Section II

The Cosmic State and Analogy of the Planets in Relationship with the Houses

Benefic Planets

1. *A benefic planet in a benefic house in good cosmic state* (planet, sign, and house have analogy) will produce the meanings of the house in great abundance, swiftly and continually through life, beginning at an early age. It also gives great protection within the realm of the meanings of the house. Example: Jupiter in Sagittarius in house two.

2. *A benefic planet in a malefic house in good cosmic state* (planet has no analogy with house) will prevent adverse events and people of the house. If the evil of the house comes to the native, this event or person will be transformed and benefit the native. Example: Venus in Taurus in house twelve. (*Transformation* occurs when the planet and house meanings are opposite in nature. It can only occur in examples two and six.)

3. *A benefic planet in a benefic house in a bad cosmic state* (prevents the native from realizing the full potential of house meanings) will realize the good of the house but on a small scale with little satisfaction and of short duration at various times throughout life. Example: Venus in Scorpio in house five.

4. *A benefic planet in a malefic house in bad cosmic state* (bad cosmic state will bring problems) will produce the adverse promises of the house but will survive and will resume life (possibly limited in some way). Example: Venus in Aries in house twelve.

Malefic Planets

5. *A malefic planet in a benefic house in good cosmic state* indicates that promises of the house will come after hard work, hindrances, and delays. Once the house promises are realized, the native can maintain them with careful oversight and planning. Example: Saturn in Capricorn in house two.

6. *A malefic planet in a benefic house in bad cosmic state* (no analogy between planet and house) is a combination that destroys all the good of the house. If the native does realize the promises of the house, the good will turn to misfortune and destroy what good has come. This is called transformation. Example: Consider Adolf Hitler, who had Saturn in Leo in house ten. He made it to the top, but this was followed by the downfall. Saturn has no analogy with house ten.

7. *A malefic planet in a malefic house in good cosmic state* (planet and house have analogy) indicates that the promise of the house will come to, and after facing problems and obstacles, the native will survive and go on with a favorable final outcome. Example: Mars in Aries in house six.

8. *A malefic planet in a malefic house in bad cosmic state* (there is analogy between house, planet, and sign) is a combination that will produce the adverse meanings of the house with great speed. Example: Mars in Taurus in house eight.

Benefic Planets

Benefic Planet in a Benefic House in Good Cosmic State

A benefic planet in a benefic house in good cosmic state will produce events of that house easy and fast, in great quantity, starting early in life.

Sun in Leo in house ten: The native will receive fame, honors, prestige, promotions, and recognition with little effort, in great quantity, and starting early in life. The reasons are:

1. The essential nature of the Sun is benefic.

2. The Sun is posited in a benefic house.

3. The Sun has natural analogy with success.

4. The Sun in Leo is domicile.

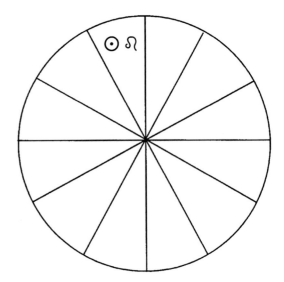

*Benefic Planet in a Benefic House
in Good Cosmic State*

Jupiter in Sagittarius in house eleven: The native will have abundant and lasting friends, who will support his or her endeavors. They will be of high position and of great benefit to the native. The reasons are:

1. The essential nature of Jupiter is benefic.

2. Jupiter is posited in a benefic house.

3. Jupiter in Sagittarius is in domicile.

4. Jupiter in good cosmic state in a benefic house will allow all the promises of the house to come to the native.

5. Jupiter has analogy with eleventh house matters.

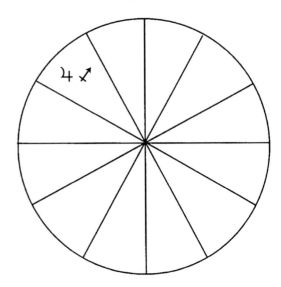

*Benefic Planet in a Benefic House
in Good Cosmic State*

26

Benefiic Planet in a Malefic House in Good Cosmic State

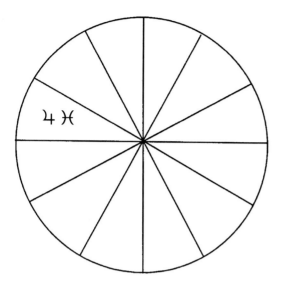

*Benefic Planet in a Malefic House
in Good Cosmic State*

Jupiter in Pisces in house twelve: The native will be protected from secret enemies, be victorious over them, or gain through them, and the health is protected. Any problems will eventually be of some benefit. The reasons are:

1. The essential nature of Jupiter is benefic.

2. Jupiter is posited in a malefic house.

3. Jupiter has no analogy with enemies or sickness.

4. Jupiter in Pisces is domicile.

5. *Transformation*: secret enemies or health issues will be transformed into something beneficial to the native.

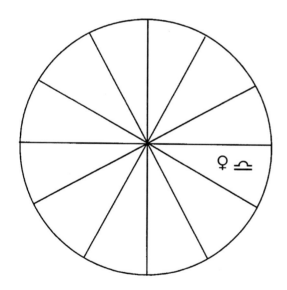

*Benefic Planet in a Malefic House
in Good Cosmic State*

Venus in Libra in house six: The native will not have any serious illness, or if he does, everything will turn out alright or will transform into something beneficial. The reasons are:

1. The essential nature of Venus is benefic.

2. Venus is posited in a malefic house.

3. Venus has no analogy with illness.

4. Venus is in domicile.

5. *Transformation*: any illness will benefit the native.

6. Any sixth house problems that occur with a benefic planet in a malefic house in good cosmic state will benefit the native in some way. This gives protection from adversity.

Benefic Planet in a Benefic House in Bad Cosmic State

Venus in Scorpio in house five: The native's love affairs leave him or her dissatisfied. Although many in number, the feeling is shallow and the duration brief, and the native is left feeling bitter. The reasons are:

1. The essential nature of Venus is benefic.

2. Venus is posited in a benefic house.

3. Venus has natural analogy with love affairs.

4. Venus in Scorpio is in detriment.

5. Determinations: Venus is in bad cosmic state.

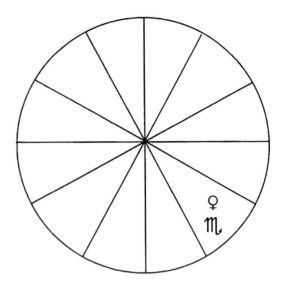

*Benefic Planet in a Benefic House
in Bad Cosmic State*

Sun in Aquarius in tenth house: The native will rise to a high position and receive honors and prestige. Upsets and some degree of difficulty will accompany success, or once achievement is realized, it could bring abrupt disappointment or disillusion. The reasons are:

1. The essential nature of the Sun is benefic.

2. The Sun is posited in a benefic house.

3. The Sun has natural analogy with fame, honors, and success.

4. The Sun in Aquarius is in detriment and bad cosmic state.

5. A benefic planet in a benefic house in bad cosmic state will realize some good of the house but for a short duration and with little satisfaction.

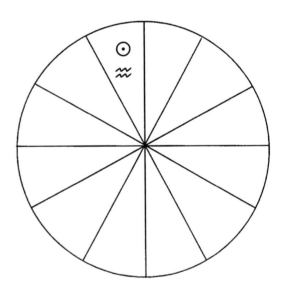

*Benefic Planet in a Benefic House
in Bad Cosmic State*

Benefic Planet in a Malefic House in Bad Cosmic State

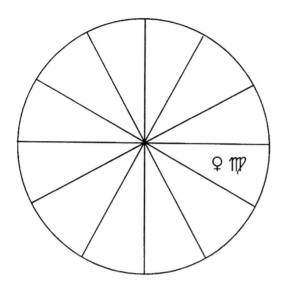

Benefic Planet in a Malefic House in Bad Cosmic State

Venus in Virgo in house six: The native will have various illnesses and ailments of a minor nature, starting early in life. The native survives and continues with life. The reasons are:

1. The essential nature of Venus is benefic.

2. Venus is posited in a malefic house.

3. Venus has no analogy with the sixth house and health problems.

4. Venus acquires analogy with the sixth by being posited in the Virgo.

5. Venus in Virgo is in fall.

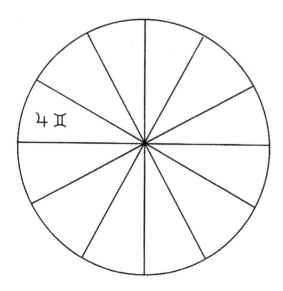

Benefic Planet in a Malefic House in Bad Cosmic State

Jupiter in Gemini in house twelve: The native will have secret enemies constantly talking behind his back, but the gossip and petty remarks will not do any lasting harm. Although the native will have bouts with illness, he or she will survive. The reasons for this are:

1. The essential nature of Jupiter is benefic.

2. Jupiter is posited in a malefic house.

3. Jupiter has no analogy with twelfth house matters.

4. Jupiter is in detriment.

5. The determinations indicate Jupiter is in bad comic state.

Malefic Planets

Malefic Planet in a Benefic House in Good Cosmic State

A malefic planet in a benefic house in good cosmic state will produce the beneficial meanings of the house, but through problems, difficulties, hard work, and delays. The good will come to the native but through sweat and tears. The promises of the house will come to the native by careful monitoring and financial planning.

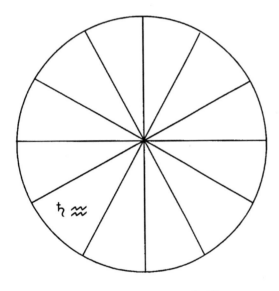

Malefic Planet in a Benefic House in Good Cosmic State

Saturn in Aquarius in house two: Money will come to the native, but through difficulties and problems and many times in an incomplete way, if the native works hard. The native will have a comfortable life. The reasons are:

1. The essential nature of Saturn is malefic.

2. Saturn is posited in a benefic house.

3. Saturn has no analogy with the second house.

4. Saturn in Aquarius is domicile.

5. Money may be difficult to obtain, but is long lasting once accumulated.

6. Saturn is in good cosmic state.

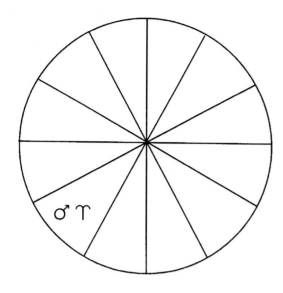

Mars in Aries in house two: The native will make money and spend a lot. He or she will always pull through any conflicts or strife in financial affairs. The reasons for this are:

1. The essential nature of Mars is malefic.

2. Mars is posited in a benefic house.

3. Mars is in its domicile.

4. The native must curb impulse buying.

5. Mars has no analogy with money.

Malefic Planet in a Benefic House in Good Cosmic State

Malefic Planet in a Benefic House in Bad Cosmic State

A malefic planet in a benefic house in bad cosmic state will prevent the attainment of the beneficial meanings of the house, or if one achieves them, they will be bad quality, mostly useless, or he or she may lose them or wish they had never been attained.

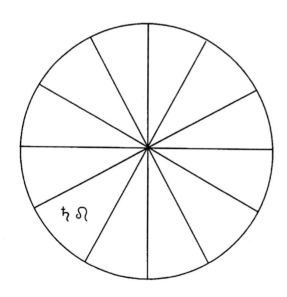

Saturn in Leo in house two: The native may not be able to obtain the money he or she desires. If money does come, it could be a source of great sorrow or the native may lose all of it. The reasons are:

1. The essential nature of Saturn is malefic.

2. Saturn is posited in a benefic house.

3. Saturn has no analogy with the house of money.

4. Saturn in Leo is in detriment.

5. *Transformation*: If the native obtains a good deal of money it will eventually impact his or her life in a negative way.

Malefic Planet in a Benefic House in Bad Cosmic State

Saturn in Cancer in house eleven: Saturn in Cancer will deny friends. If the native acquires a close friend, *transformation* occurs. In some way the friend will be removed, such as through a long-distance move or an unforeseen circumstance. There is sadness. The reasons are:

1. The essential nature of Saturn is malefic.

2. Saturn is posited in a benefic house.

3. Saturn has no analogy with friendships.

4. Saturn in Cancer is in detriment.

5. *Transformation*: If the native obtains a friend, the situation eventually will cause sadness or problems.

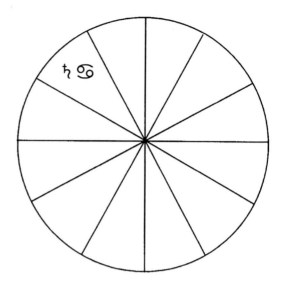

*Malefic Planet in a Benefic House
in Bad Cosmic State*

Malefic Planet in a Malefic House in Good Cosmic State

A malefic planet in a malefic house in good cosmic state will not stop the adverse meanings of the house, but in the final outcome, one will be free from them.

Saturn in Capricorn in house six: The native will have an illness of a serious nature, but the outcome will be alright. He or she may develop a chronic condition, but it will not be disabling. The reasons are:

1. The essential nature of Saturn is a malefic.

2. Saturn is posited in a malefic house.

3. Saturn has analogy with illness.

4. Saturn is in domicile.

5. Other determinations: good cosmic state.

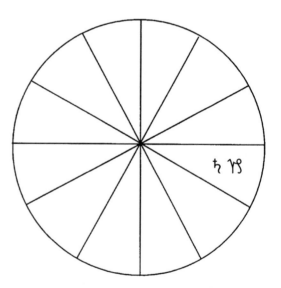

*Malefic Planet in a Malefic House
in Good Cosmic State*

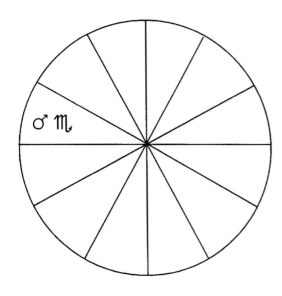

Mars in Scorpio in house twelve: Beginning early in life the native will have secret enemies who gossip and cause problems. Illness and even surgery are indicated. The native is victorious over all of these problems even though the situations are unpleasant. The reasons are:

1. The essential nature of Mars is malefic.

2. Mars is posited in a malefic house.

3. Mars has analogy with enemies and illness in the twelfth house.

4. Mars is domicile.

5. Determinations: good cosmic state.

Malefic Planet in a Malefic House
in Good Cosmic State

Malefic Planet in a Malefic House in Bad Cosmic State

A malefic planet in a malefic house in bad cosmic state will produce in great speed the adverse meanings of the house.

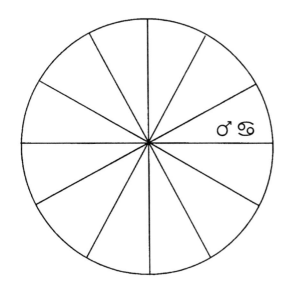

Mars in Cancer in house seven: The native will have open enemies, conflicts and arguments, with little effort on his or her part. Starting early in life, the enemies will attack when least expected and they will crop up throughout life. The reasons are:

1. The essential nature of Mars is malefic.

2. Mars is posited in a partly malefic house.

3. Mars has great analogy with enemies.

4. Mars is in fall.

5. Other determinations: bad cosmic state.

Malefic Planet in a Malefic House
in Bad Cosmic State

Saturn in Leo in house twelve: Powerful secret enemies may attempt to evoke misfortune on the native. They will attempt to hinder, oppose, obstruct, and stimulate all kinds of difficulties. Health issues occur throughout life, including possible heart problems. Twelfth house matters begin at an early age. The reasons are:

1. The essential nature of Saturn is malefic.

2. Saturn is posited in a malefic house.

3. Saturn has analogy with enemies, illness, and the meanings of house twelve.

4. Saturn is in detriment.

5. Other determinations: bad cosmic state.

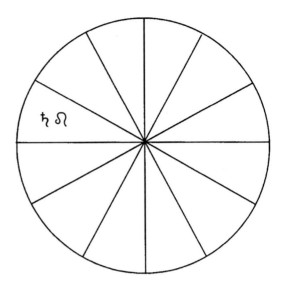

Malefic Planet in a Malefic House in Bad Cosmic State

Dispositor

The disposer of a planet is the ruler of the sign this planet occupies. If Saturn is in Sagittarius, its disposer is Jupiter. If Jupiter is in Libra, its disposer is Venus. A planet never acts without the cooperation of the sign it is located in. If it is not in its own sign (domicile), it will act according to the nature and state of its ruler. In fact, many times the planet will act according to the dispositor's location.

The influence of a planet can be changed due to this alteration of its essential nature by the disposer. When a planet is not in its own sign, one should ascertain if and how it is connected with its disposer, and determine the state of both. When a planet is in conjunction or aspect with its disposer, it will be more directly ruled by it.

Morin states the following: A planet in its fall loses its strength; the character of its force, nevertheless, depends on: (1) the planet's own nature (benefic or malefic), (2) the nature and cosmic state of its disposer, and (3) the essential nature of the sign the planet occupies. As an example, the effect of Saturn in Aries, in the sign of its fall, is unfavorable because of its own malefic nature; and its disposer, Mars, is equally malefic because of its cooperation with Aries. The effect of the Moon in Scorpio is malefic (fall) because Mars, the disposer of the Moon and ruler of Scorpio, is a malefic.

General Rules for Determining the Effect of Dispositors

1. A planet will depend more on its dispositor and be more directly ruled by it, when in conjunction or aspect with it.

2. If the planet in question is in bad cosmic state or located in a malefic house, but its disposer is in good cosmic state, events and matters will go badly in the beginning, but take a turn for the better, especially if approaching a good aspect with its dispositor.

3. If the planet is in good cosmic state, but its dispositor is in a bad one, the success at the beginning will turn into failure or bring some sadness; the project may have to be abandoned.

4. When both planets are in good cosmic state and in a benefic house, something fortunate will result.

5. When both planets are in good cosmic state and in a malefic house, something adverse will be lessened or suppressed.

6. When both planets are in bad cosmic state, they will destroy or limit any advantages of the house, if in a benefic house.

7. When both planets are in bad cosmic state and in a malefic house, they produce trouble and loss.

8. A planet that is in a sign other than its own and is in harmony with its dispositor by nature, position or analogy, achieves the effects, which are considerable.

9. Each planet acts according to its essential nature, its house position, and cosmic state.

10. Determination should only be applied to the physical (house) position of the dispositor, and not the houses ruled by the dispositor.

Dispositor Example 1

The Sun in Pisces in house four is disposed by Jupiter in house twelve. The Sun will act:

1. By virtue of rulership in house nine.

2. In house four, where it is placed.

The Sun will act in house twelve where its dispositor is located. The Sun will not influence the meanings of house one, where Jupiter rules.

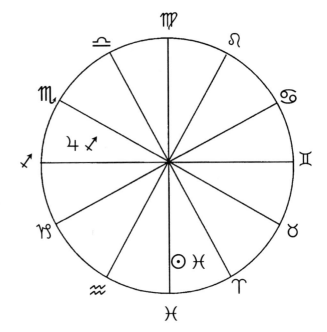

Dispositor Example 1

Dispositor Example 2

Venus is in Pisces in house three, disposed by Jupiter in house one. Venus will act on the meanings of house one, but not on the meanings of house twelve, where Jupiter rules.

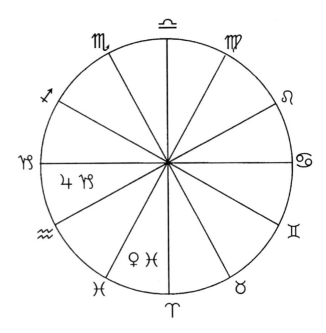

Dispositor Example 2

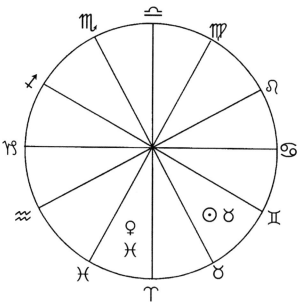

Dispositor Example 3

Dispositor Example 3

The Sun is in Taurus in house five, disposed by Venus in Pisces in house three. The Sun can only be determined for house five, where it is located; for house eight, where it is co-ruler; and for house three, the position of its dispositor.

Dispositor Example 4

The Sun in Aries in house one is disposed by Mars in Capricorn in house ten. The native will achieve honors or an illustrious position, attended with some danger.

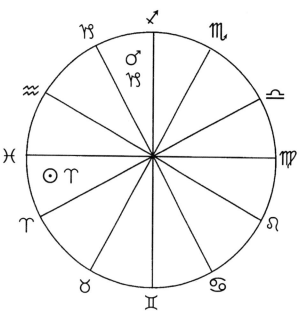

Dispositor Example 4

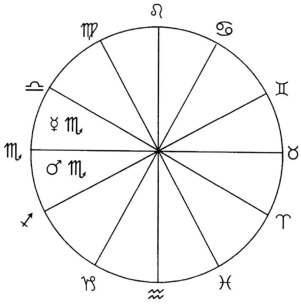

Dispositor Example 5

Dispositor Example 5

Mercury in Scorpio in house twelve is disposed by Mars in house one. Having analogy with intellect, Mercury will act by reason of its disposer in house one. Mercury in house one imparts a fine intellect.

Note: The force of a peregrine planet depends on the antagonism or agreement between the nature of its disposer and its own nature.

Peregrine Planets

If a planet is not in the sign of its dignity, dibility, or triplicity, it is said to be peregrine. The degree of its effect is determined by the planet's own nature and the gender of its sign position. When the planet is in the sign of its own gender, it will always act more favorably. Next, the planet's disposer and its sign position should be analyzed. The planet is somewhat corrupted if posited in a sign of an antagonistic disposer; for example, Mercury in Scorpio, ruled by Mars in Taurus (detriment). But if Mercury were in Cancer, ruled by the Moon in Taurus (exaltation), the effect would be much better.

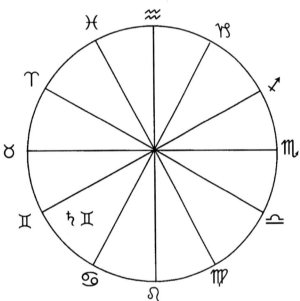

Peregrine Planets Example 1

Peregrine Planets Example 1

Saturn in house two in peregrine neither gives nor destroys wealth, but if the native does receive money, he or she may not be able to hold on to it except by excessive economy and cleverness concerning savings.

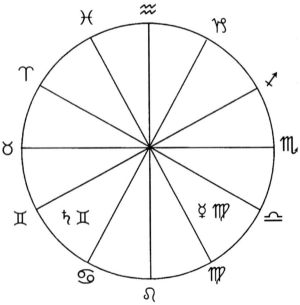

Peregrine Planets Example 2

Peregrine Planets Example 2

Saturn is in house two in Gemini, and Mercury is the disposer of Saturn and in house five in Virgo (domicile), so the native will have to exert some effort and frugality in order to hold onto money. Thrifty habits will benefit the native financially. Someone assists the native with a savings plan and secure investments.

Peregrine Planets Example 3

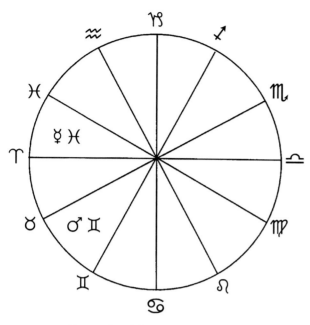

Peregrine Planets Example 3

Mars in Gemini in house two in peregrine is disposed by Mercury in house twelve in Pisces (fall). Mars rules houses one and eight. Mars has no analogy with money and its dispositor is posited in the house of loss and sorrow (fall.) This will threaten the finances through deception and/or fraud as well as unwise decisions. Health issues are costly and prolonged, possibly because of incorrect diagnoses. Any inheritance received could be a threat to life. The reasons are:

1. The essential nature of Mars is malefic.

2. Mars rules the Ascendant and the malefic eighth.

3. Mars has no analogy with money.

4. The disposer of Mars is Mercury in fall.

5. Mercury is posited in a malefic house.

6. Mercury in fall in house twelve has analogy with theft and fraud.

7. Mars is a masculine planet in a masculine sign, which is good; but the disposer of Mars is posited in a feminine sign.

8. Mars, by being posited in house two, and by reason of the opposition to house eight, acquires an accidental signification of the meanings of house eight.

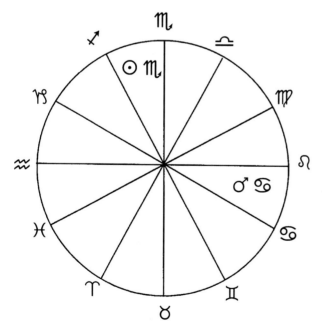

Peregrine Planets Example 4

Peregrine Planets Example 4

The Sun in Scorpio in house ten is in peregrine, disposed by Mars in Cancer in house six, and Mars is in its fall in a malefic house. The Sun in the tenth has analogy with honors and success, and Mars in Cancer in the sixth with illness. The high position and success of the native will bring a difficult illness.

Determination Through House Position and Rulership

Determining Possible Combinations

The house meanings represent the events, circumstances, people, experiences, and the possibilities in the life of the native. The planets materialize these matters. Consequently, it is necessary to first determine a combination whose realization is materially possible.

Combinations Example 1

The ruler of house ten is in house five. It is impossible for the father of the native to also be his child. It is possible for the father to bring happiness to the child as this is a combination whose realization is possible.

A planet ruling one house but located in another indicates certain events by reason of its rulership and another set of events due to its location. The combinations of meanings come

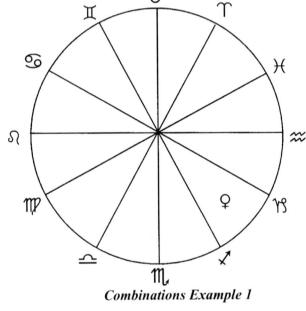

Combinations Example 1

true in a beneficial or adverse way according to the nature, analogy, and cosmic state of the planet in question.

Combinations Example 2

The ruler of house two is in house seven. The planet itself, as it is a benefic in domicile, indicates something good regarding marriage, lawsuits, and contracts. As ruler of house two, it could be something good regarding money. The realization of matters can be separate or in mutual combination.

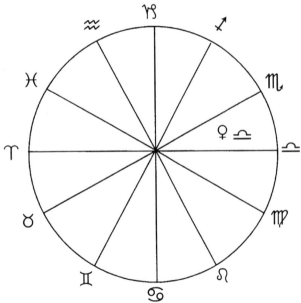

Combinations Example 2

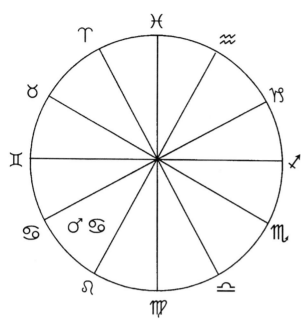

Combinations Example 3

Combinations Example 3

The ruler of house eleven is in house two. There is no analogy with Mars in fall in the house of money, which is an indication of something adverse for finances. As the ruler of friends, there can be something adverse in those matters as well. As the ruler of house six of health, there is an indication of health problems. The combination of friends and illness causing heavy debts is a realization that is materially possible.

Friends, servants, and employees cause heavy losses, and debts are incurred through illness.

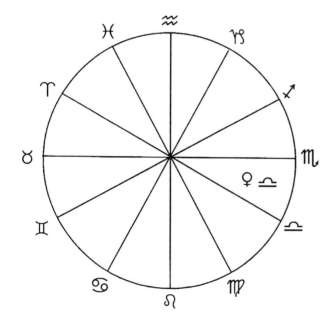

Combinations Example 4

Combinations Example 4

Fortunate things from employees, servants, and pets, and happiness in daily work.

41

Combinations Example 5

Problems and danger from servants, employees, small animals. Serious health problems, and reckless behavior can bring a brush with death. This is an example of a malefic planet in bad cosmic state in a malefic house.

When combining, always consider the meanings of the house and the ruler. The possibilities whose nature most agrees with the nature, analogy, and cosmic state will have the greatest possibility of realization.

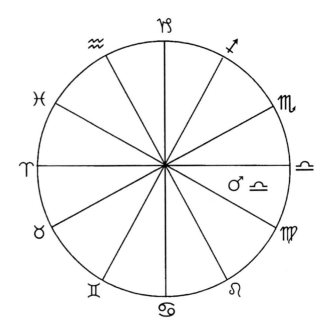

Combinations Example 5

Combinations Example 6

The ruler of house ten is in house twelve. The meanings of house ten will affect the meanings of house twelve or vice-versa. But a planet is more strongly determined by position than by its rulership. Saturn is a malefic, located in a malefic house in bad cosmic state. Professional activities or reputation will be the cause of illness, secret enemies, sorrow, and loss. Friends become enemies when the ruler of house eleven is in house twelve. This is an example of a malefic planet in bad cosmic state in a maleific house. Saturn in its fall has analogy with house twelve matters.

Always carefully analyze the essential nature of the planet in question, and its analogy or antagonism with the house in question.

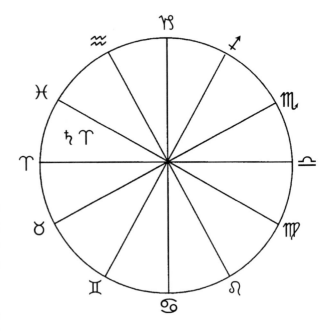

Combinations Example 6

Combinations Example 7

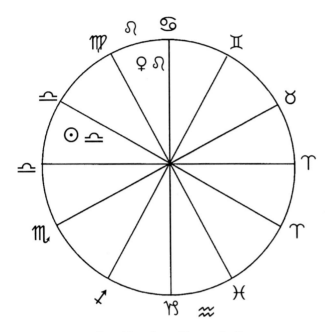

Combinations Example 7

Venus, ruler of houses one and twelve, is posited in house ten. The ruler of house twelve is a benefic, and in the sign of Leo acquires analogy with honors and success, and even more so as ruler of the Ascendant. The twelfth house will be a starting point for success or recognition.

Confinement, illness, sorrow, or secret activities and enemies will lead the native to remarkable undertakings that bring some success.

The location and state of the dispositor would have much to do with the degree of success. If the Sun happens to be in fall, a number of setbacks are indicated.

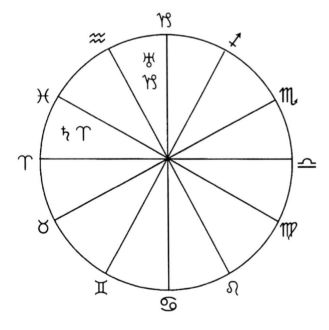

Combinations Example 8

Combinations Examples 8 and 9

In example 8, the ruler of house ten is in the twelfth, and the ruler of house eleven is in the tenth. Friends will assist the native in the career, but the native's actions in professional activities could cause many friends to become secret enemies. It could also indicate that the high position of the native is a source of sorrow, or the native may give up honors or high rank due to unhappiness with the profession. Uranus in house ten indicates abrupt elevation and abrupt descent.

If the planet ruling house ten is malefic, in detriment or fall, and receives bad aspects, the native could go to prison for his or her unethical enterprises. When a planet rules a house but is located in a house whose meanings are opposite, the significations of the house deprived of its ruler are passed to those of the house where its ruler is located.

In Example 9, the ruler of house twelve is posited in house seven. House twelve is secret enemies, and house seven is open enemies. Mars rules and is posited in the sign of its fall. Secret enemies come out in the open to attack the native. Any behind the scenes activities or matters of a secret nature are also dangerous and usually discovered. Both houses rule enemies, but the opposition in the nature of secret and open enemies can be very detrimental when connected by a malefic in bad cosmic state.

Analogy between houses five and twelve indicates secret love affairs, and in this combination a secret love affair that can cause the marriage partner to threaten divorce.

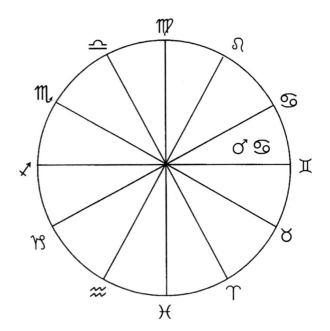

Combinations Example 9

Determining Cause and Effect

When a planet is present in one house and rules another, the meanings of house position and house rulership can be combined if the nature of the planet agrees. When an analogy exists between the ruled house and the planet, it will bring tangible results. A logical affinity should exist between the houses. In fact, the greater the analogy, the greater the probability that matters will be realized.

The realization of the affairs will materialize in a favorable or unfavorable way according to the essential nature and cosmic state of the planet and its agreement or antagonism with the house in question. Therefore, close attention should be paid to the character of the house, including the various meanings, as combination will be possible when the essential nature of the planet agrees.

Once the possible combinations are determined, the rule of cause-and-effect should be mastered. Study this rule carefully, refer to it often, use it wisely.

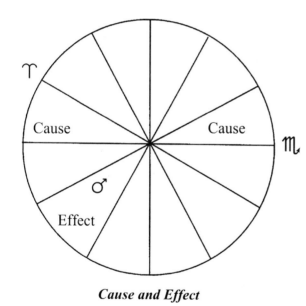

Cause and Effect

Cause and Effect

1. The house position of the planet is the effect.

2. The house the planet rules is the cause or origin.

3. Combination is possible when the essential nature of the planet agrees with the house it is in or houses it rules.

45

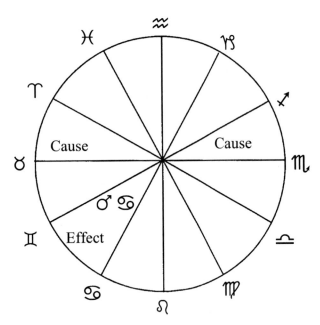

Cause and Effect Example 1

Cause and Effect Example 1

Mars is in Cancer in house two and rules houses seven and twelve. Combination is possible as the essential nature of Mars has analogy with the meanings of the houses over which it rules.

Possible combinations:

1. Houses two and seven: money and partnerships, lawsuits, open enemies.

2. Houses two and twelve: money and illness, secret enemies, confinement.

3. Houses two, seven, and twelve: Partnerships, lawsuits, thieves, illness, confinment, and money.

The native may not obtain financial success or any realization of money will bring a threat of loss. His riches could be lost because of partnerships, theft, lawsuits, enemies, illness, theives, or confinement.

The position of the planet is the effect: second house of money. The cause is the houses ruled by Mars: seven and twelve. Combination is possible as the nature of Mars (malefic) agrees with meanings of the houses it rules. Mars has great affinity and analogy with enemies, robbers, theft, confrontations, and loss. Mars is in Cancer (fall) and posited in the second—no analogy with financial gain. Any realization of money will bring a possibility of loss.

Cause and effect is only an expression of a few essesital factors of a whole series. Unquestionably, there are no formulas of fixed application. The final judgment should always be based on all the factors in the nativity.

On the other hand, the horoscope taken as a whole does not cause a specific event or quality. It is the planets that denote certain qualities and future events and the extent and nature of these events. As we go through the various examples, keep in mind that there are many possible combinations and limited space here.

In determining cause and effect, always consider:

1. The planets' analogy with the houses that are being judged.

2. Which house meanings most agree with the planet.

3. The cosmic state of the planet.

4. The house position of the planet is the effect.

5. The house the planet rules is the cause.

6. The house position and house rulership may combine when there is analogy.

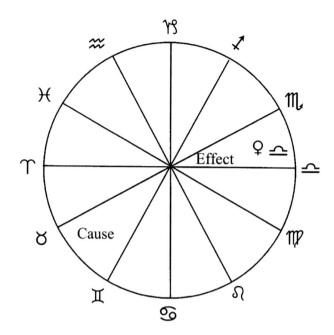

Cause and Effect Example 2

Example 2

The finances of the native contributed to the happy state of marriage. She attracts business and marriage partners who increase her financial security.

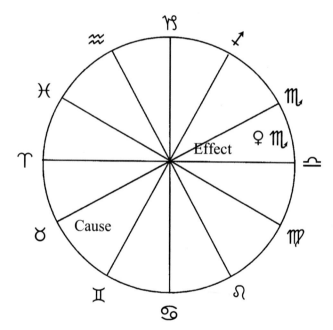

Cause and Effect Example 3

Example 3

The native's financial problems increase with marriage. Although stress and arguments regarding money will be common, the native will never be destitute.

The essential nature of the planet will always prevail, but the manifestation will be strengthened or weakened by the cosmic state. The cosmic state determines if the planet will be a help or hindrance in matters pertaining to the house.

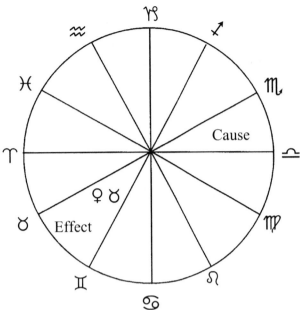

Cause and Effect Example 4

Example 4

Increase in wealth due to marriage, partnerships, or lawsuits.

Example 5

Brothers or sisters cause heavy debts, or dangerous auto accident causes excessive loss and major debt.

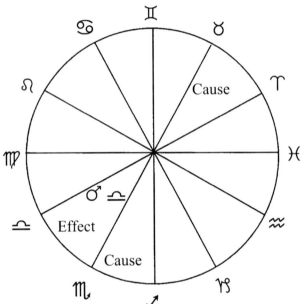

Cause and Effect Example 5

Example 6

Brothers or sisters help in the success of the native. The native's brilliant mind assured his success and high position. The Sun is in Aries and exalted in house ten where there is analogy. The Sun rules house three.

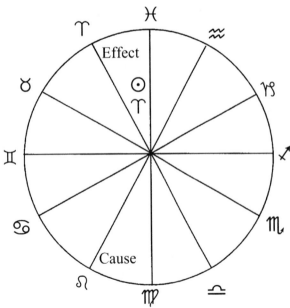

Cause and Effect Example 6

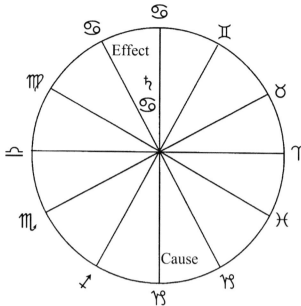

Cause and Effect Example 7

Example 7

Parents help in the native's ascent to success, but with success comes sorrow, loss, and downfall.

Example 8

With a good public reputation the native attracts a respectable, financially secure partner, and together they make a fortune. Jupiter in Cancer is exalted, and rules houses seven and ten.

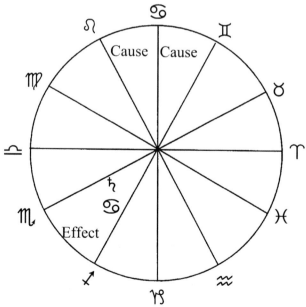

Cause and Effect Example 9

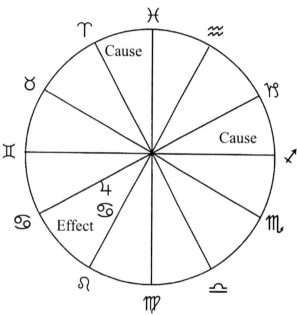

Cause and Effect Example 8

Example 9

A fortune is lost from a badly conducted enterprise.

The position or ruler of a planet in a house indicates that an event may or may not happen to the native. The materialization is decided by the planets nature, analogy, and cosmic state.

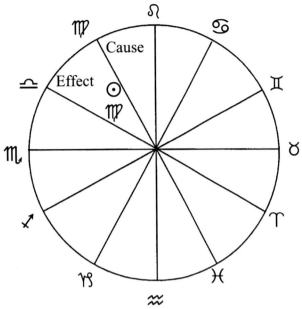

Cause and Effect Example 10

Example 10
The profession will bring friends of prominence with intellectual capabilities. The Sun has analogy with success and prominence.

Cause and Effect Example 11
Friends will assist in the native's achievement of success and prestige. Because the Leo Sun is in domicile in house ten, it guarantees success, and has great analogy with matters of house ten.

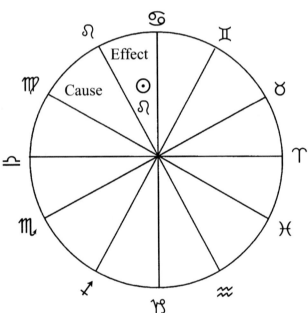

Cause and Effect Example 11

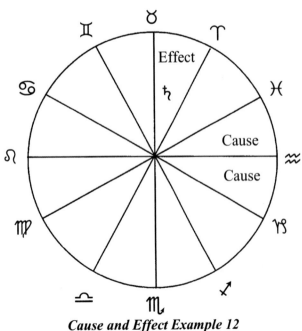

Cause and Effect Example 12

Example 12
Travel caused an illness. Saturn rules house six and co-rules house seven. When a planet rules two houses, these meanings can blend with and influence the house where the planet is located. A partner, lawsuit, enemy, or an illness may cause the native to travel.

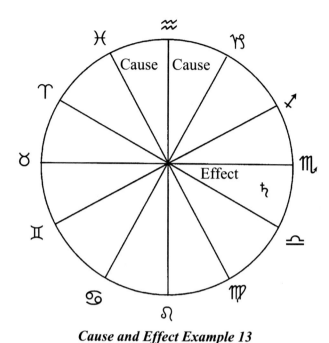

Cause and Effect Example 13

Example 13

In example 13, Saturn is placed in house six and rules houses nine and ten. A logical determination would be: the native will travel due to professional enterprises, and this results in an illness. Another logical analysis would be: prolonged mental stress of professional endeavors resulted in a chronic or serious illness. (Much depends on the cosmic state of Saturn).

Saturn has no analogy with travel, but great analogy with illness. Also, Saturn has analogy with the intellect, mentality, and studies. It produces a serious and profound mind in the first, third, or ninth, especially when in good cosmic state and receiving good aspects.

The most powerful of the determining factors is the physical position of the planet, followed by rulership and aspects. Each planet always acts conjointly with the sign it is in. In addition it provokes one thing due to its house position, and another thing because of its rulership in another house.

The malefics can cause exceedingly good things when in domicile or exaltation. Obviously, they produce these benefits if they are located in or ruling benefic houses. Their constructive action, however, is usually attended with difficulties, frustration, and stress.

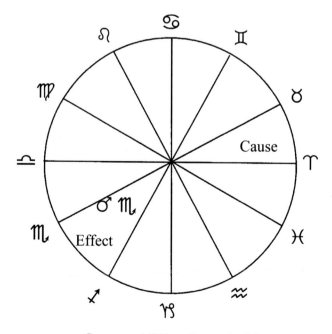

Cause and Effect Example 14

Example 14

Financial gain from war, lawsuits, confrontations.

Mars is in Scorpio in house two, and rules house seven. Mars is domicile. Money will come to the native, but it will take hard work. Endurance through stress will raise the native to higher levels.

A planet in its own sign will act in a complete, powerful, and benefic way. It is even more beneficial if the planet has analogy with the affairs of the house. Mars is inclined to spend, so careful budgeting is a must.

Example 15

Mars in Capricorn is exalted in house seven and rules houses five and ten. A love affair causes disruption in a business partnership or marriage. A parent and a child will interfere in a business partnership or marriage. Professional activities bring aggressive open enemies forward, but the native eludes their threats.

Mars in exaltation acquires great power. Problems conclude in the native's favor, but there is a price to pay. The nature and state of the dispositor will help or hinder the outcome.

When a planet rules two houses, at times the three houses combine and at other times only two combine.

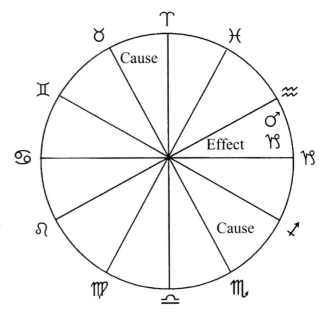

Cause and Effect Example 15

Example 16

Friends gave the native the financial and emotional support he needed to succeed. (Siblings did not help.) Sometimes all houses combine and at other times they do not.

Mercury rules houses two, three, and eleven, and is located in house ten. Mercury in Taurus has analogy with money, and is also clever in business. Mercury is peregrine and its dispositor Venus and its determinations must be examined.

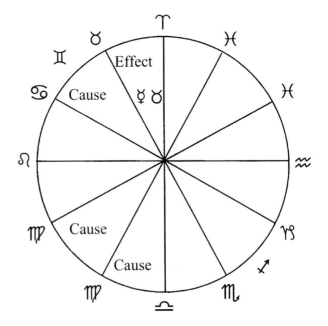

Cause and Effect Example 16

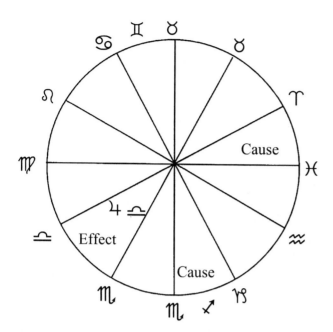

Cause and Effect Example 17

Example 17

Wealth came with marriage as well as from inheritance.

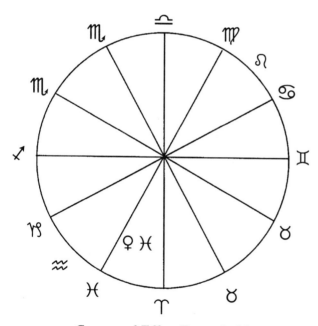

Cause and Effect Example 18

Example 18

Venus in Pisces is exalted, which is a benefic planet in a benefic house in good cosmic state. The native's success in life was due to faithful and loyal employees. Neither a parent nor his children were involved in his success.

Determining Combination by Analogy

When a planet rules a house but is located in a house whose meanings are opposite, the significations of the house deprived of its ruler are passed to those of the house where the ruler is located.

Example 1

Mars, ruler of house two of gain, is posited in the house of loss. Mars has no analogy with money.

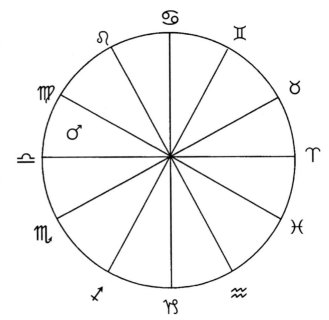

Example 1, Determining Combination by Analogy

Example 2

Mars, ruler of the house of death, is posited in the house of life. Mars has analogy with death.

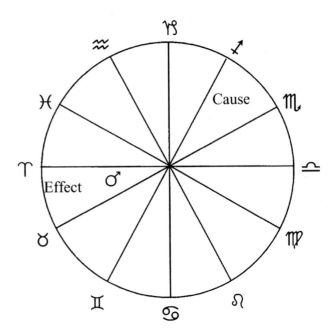

Example 2, Determining Combination by Analogy

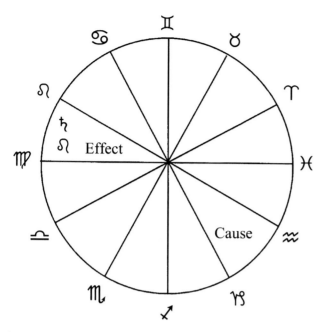

Example 3, Determining Combination by Analogy

Example 3

this is an example of a malefic planet in a malefic house in detriment. Saturn, ruler of house five of love, passion, and children, is posited in house twelve of sorrow and loss. The native was heartbroken because of lost love, a child caused much sadness, and the strain of the situation resulted in ill health as Saturn also rules house six. When a malefic planet is in one house and rules another with opposite meaning, the effect is powerful to undo the good of the benefic house.

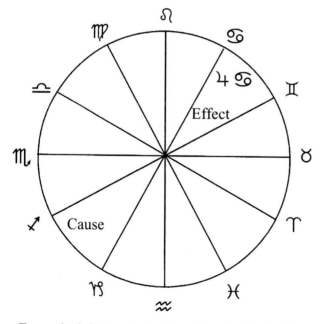

Example 4, Determining Combination by Analogy

Example 4

Jupiter, ruler of the house of money, is posited in the house of inheritance. Jupiter has analogy with money, even more so in exaltation. The meanings of houses two and eight correspond as far as money and inheritance are concerned. The native would receive a large inheritance. There is analogy between planet and house rulership.

Example 5

Venus, ruler of house two, is in house eight. Venus also has analogy with money, but is posited in Aries, the sign of its detriment. Venus acquires analogy with the adverse meanings of house eight. Any inheritance could bring an element of danger to the native.

Benefic planets have analogy with benefic houses. Benefic planets acquire analogy with malefic houses by sign, dispositor, and aspect. The nature of Venus is benefic, and the essential nature always prevails, but in the sign of detriment and located in house eight, the quality is greatly weakened.

Always consider the analogies that exist between a planet, the sign it is in, and its house position as well as the houses it rules.

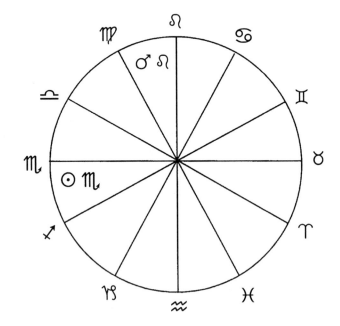

Example 5, Determining Combination by Analogy

Example 6

A military career.

Example 6, Determining Combination by Analogy

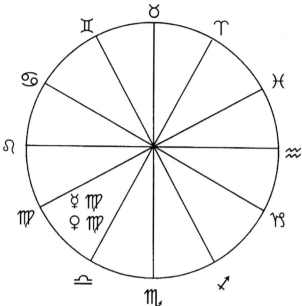

Example 7, Determining Combination by Analogy

Example 7

Financial gain through a medical career. It is always powerful if the planet is in a house and sign whose meanings have analogy to the meanings of the house it rules.

Example 8

The seventh is the house of marriage. Venus, ruler of house five (house of love), is located in house seven in Leo (sign of love). The houses, the planet, and the sign all have analogy, and are very powerful.

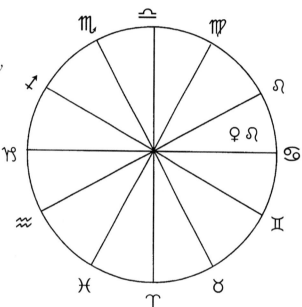

Example 8, Determining Combination by Analogy

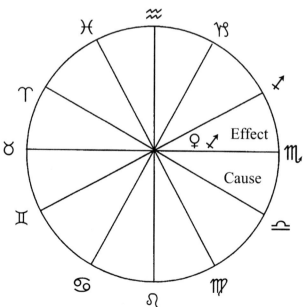

Example 9, Determining Combination by Analogy

Example 9

The native married his employee. This has analogy.

57

Example 10

An employee filed a lawsuit against the native.

In both examples 9 and 10, the ruler of house six is in house seven. In example 9, Venus is ruler and has great analogy with love and marriage and is posited in the house of marriage. In example 10, the ruler of house six is Mars. Mars has no analogy with love and marriage. But great analogy exists between Mars and confrontations, threats, enemies, and lawsuits.

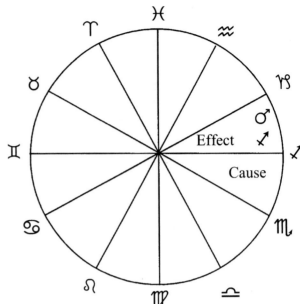

Example 10, Determining Combination by Analogy

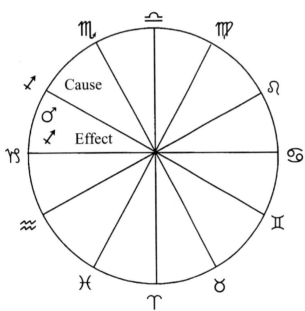

Example 11, Determining Combination by Analogy

Example 11

With the ruler of house eleven in house twelve friends become enemies in this example of a malefic planet in a malefic house.

Example 12

With the ruler of house twelve in house eleven, enemies become friends in this example of a benefic planet in a benefic house.

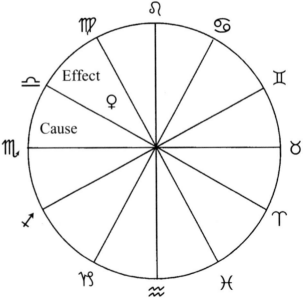

Example 12, Determining Combination by Analogy

58

When Planets Are Conjunct

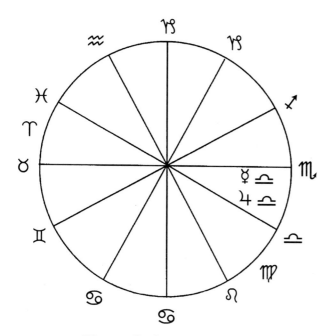

Planets Conjunct Example 1

Careful attention must be paid to any planet that is conjunct another planet. A planet can be determined by this other planet in the direction of its position or rulership. These combinations and determinations contain the principle secrets of astrological judgments. In considering the two planets together, note the houses they rule.

Example 1

The ruler of house two conjunct Jupiter promises money.

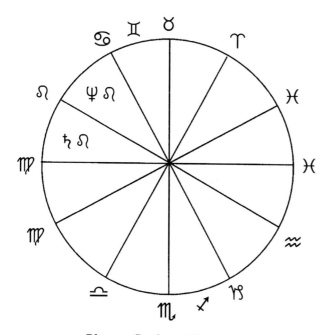

Planets Conjunct Example 2

Example 2

The ruler of house six conjunct the ruler of house eight indicates a serious illness.

Example 3

The ruler of house one conjunct the ruler of house eight in house three: a serious accident.

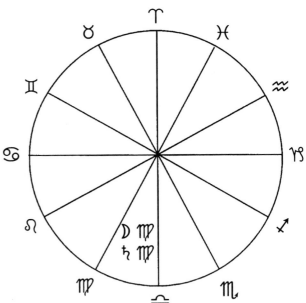

Planets Conjunct Example 3

Example 4

The ruler of house two conjunct the ruler of house eleven in house ten: money and recognition through initiative and personal efforts. Note: Venus is in domicile, and Saturn is exalted.

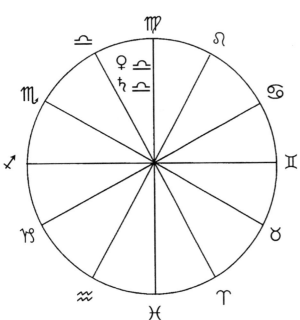

Planets Conjunct Example 4

Example 5

The ruler of house one is conjunct the ruler of houses ten and eleven: success in the profession with a friend. Jupiter is besieged by two malefics, and the business eventually ended abruptly.

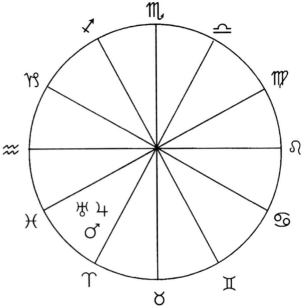

Planets Conjunct Example 5

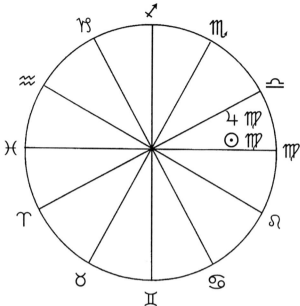

Planets Conjunct Example 6

Example 6

The ruler of the Ascendant conjunct the Sun, ruler of house six: a marriage or partnership with a physician or other healthcare professional.

Example 7

The ruler of house twelve is conjunct the ruler of house three. The native's brother is a secret enemy. The brother also interferes in the marriage.

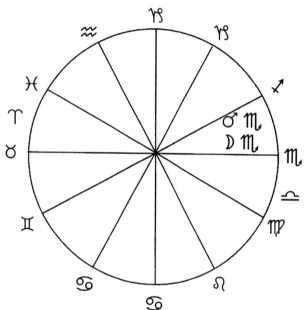

Planets Conjunct Example 7

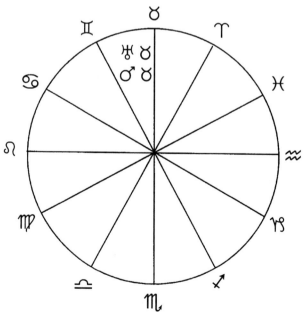

Planets Conjunct Example 8

Example 8

The ruler of house nine is conjunct the ruler of house seven. The native's beliefs cause open enemies who damage the professional career, home life, and marriage. This is an example of Mars in Detriment conjunct Uranus.

Always consider the essential nature of the planets.

Example 9

The ruler of houses seven, two, ten, and five are conjunct in house three. The native's career, open enemies, finances, love affairs, and search for pleasure destroyed his mind. Money losses caused mental instability.

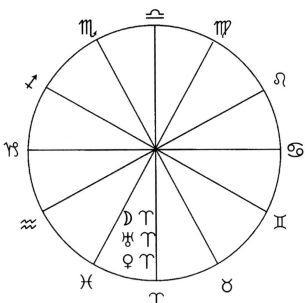

Planets Conjunct Example 9

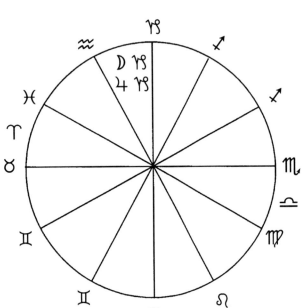

Planets Conjunct Example 10

Example 10

The ruler of houses eight, nine, and twelve is conjunct the ruler of house four. Conditions surrounding the end of life will involve a foreign country, travel, politics, secret enemies, and career.

Example 11

The co-ruler of house seven is conjunct the ruler of houses nine and four. The native moved to a foreign country to be with her partner during his exile.

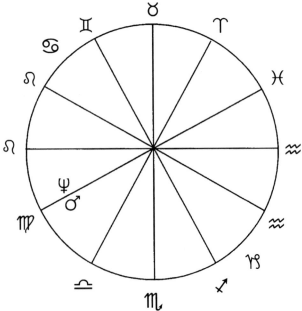

Planets Conjunct Example 11

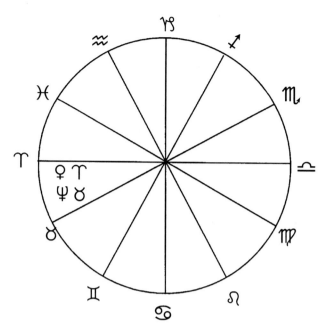

Example 12

The ruler of house twelve conjunct the ruler of house seven: secret sorrow through marriage.

Planets Conjunct Example 12

63

Section III

Determination by Actual Location

If a single planet is located in a given house, the action of that planet will exert a great influence on matters of that house. Since house position is stronger than rulership, this planet will have more influence than planets ruling or sending aspects.

The planet's nature and the house meanings should be ascertained to determine if analogy exists. A planet whose nature has some analogy to the meaning of the house it occupies will grant those matters unless strongly prevented in some other way. If the planet's nature is contrary to the meanings of the house, the planet will deny, remove, or limit the matters pertaining to that house.

Benefic planets are constructive and produce benefits; they are inclined to give the good things in life. This good can also consist in the turning away of harm. Malefics, however, are destructive; they are inclined to give the things in life one does not want. They usually indicate matters that are accompanied by accidents, surgery, danger or difficulties, or cause the matter to be imperfect. This harm can also occur by destroying any benefits already received.

Since the planets denote a certain kind of quality or a future event and its extent and nature, a determination must be made as to how the planet in question will act.

A Single Planet in a House

In order of strength, a planet acts:

1. In the house in which it is placed. Here it has the most influence.
2. In the house it rules, and sometimes through rulership by exaltation.
3. In the house to which it sends an aspect.
4. In the house where its dispositor is placed.
5. In the house ruled by a planet in aspect.

To determine if this planet will realize the matters of the house in question, prevent them, limit them, destroy what was realized, or make them a source of fortuue or misfortune, is determined by the nature of the planet and its determinations.

When several planets are found in a house, each planet must be considered by its essential nature, cosmic state, analogy, and other determinations. Many planets in one house is an indication of something extraodinary in the matters pertaining to that house.

Each planet will act according to its own nature and determinations, but if one has more analogy with the matters of the house than the others, this planet has the greatest capacity to realize or destroy the benefits or adversities of the house.

The planet closest to the cusp of the house should be examined, as this planet is very powerful with respect to the meanings of the house.

Other factors to consider when making a judgment are:

1. The planet which is also the house ruler will be powerful; next most powerful is a planet in exaltation; and last, the planet having the closest natural analogy with the house meanings.

2. Examine the dispositor of the group of planets. This dispositor's significations will form the point of departure for whatever fortune or misfortune is produced by the group of planets.

3. Consider the essential nature of the group of planets and their dignity or debility by sign. A powerful planet always conquers the weaker one.

4. Each planet in the house should be examined by its nature, analogy, cosmic state, and local determinations (house position and rulership).

Always give careful consideration to the analogical meanings of any conjunction or stellium

Example of Analogical Meanings
Powerful hidden enemies can damage the native's reputation. Mercury, ruler of houses one and ten, is conjunct the Sun, ruler of house twelve. Consideration should be given to the determinations of the Sun.

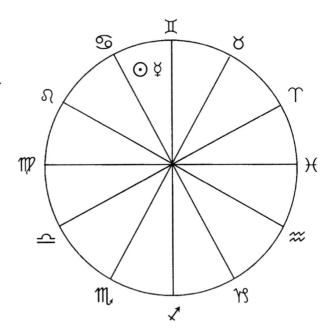

Example of Analogical Meanings

68

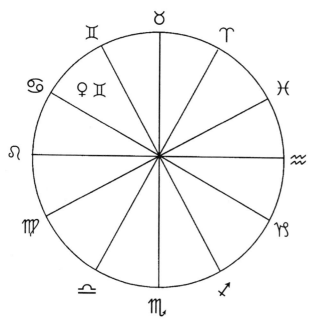

*Chart 1: Venus in the Eleventh House
and House Rulerships*

Chart 1: Venus will act first in the house in which it is placed as here it has the strongest influence. The native has numerous acquaintances but only a few who are close. There are many phone calls, letters, and trips to see the friends as there is great understanding and exchange of ideas. Friends are youthful, charming, attractive, clever, and chatty.

Venus will act next in the houses it rules: three and ten. The native will gain by travel, relatives, and communication, and achieve accomplishments through art, music, writing, speaking, and ideas. Success in life will be due to these talents.

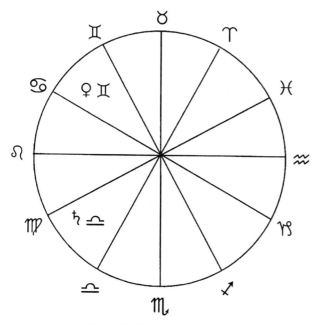

Chart 2: Venus in Aspect

Chart 2: Venus is trine Saturn from houses eleven to two. Saturn gains analogy with money by being in Libra and also by its good aspect to Venus. Money will come to the native through many endeavors, but the native will have to work hard as this is the nature of Saturn. (Saturn is exalted in Libra.) Saturn rules houses six and seven, so the possibility of a working partnership with a friend is strongly suggested. Saturn trine Venus also suggests a few older and wise friends.

Chart 3: Venus acts in the house to which it sends an aspect. The native forms a business partnership with a friend, and the partner benefits from the native's friends.

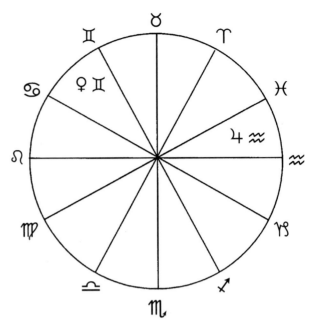

Chart 3: Native's Partner Benefits from Friends

Chart 4: Venus acts in the house where its dispositor is placed. Venus is disposed by Mercury in Taurus in house nine. The native has friends in foreign countries, and travels to see them often. There are exchanges of letters and paperwork as well as phone calls. A business partnership is established with a friend overseas, Mercury in Taurus suggests this partnershp will be financially successful.

A planet acts:
1. House position.
2. House of rulership.
3. Exaltation.
4. Dispositor.
5. Aspect.

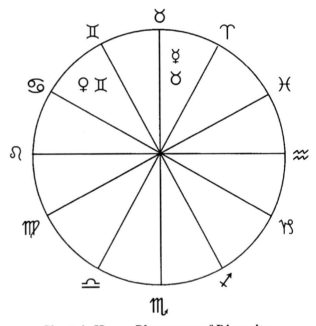

Chart 4: House Placement of Dispositor

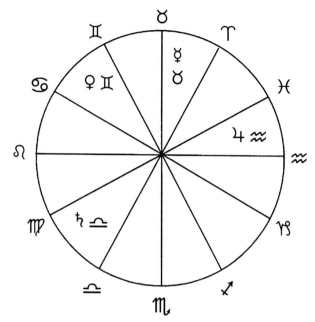

Chart 5: Venus acts in the house ruled by a planet in aspect. Venus is trine Jupiter, with Sagittarius on the cusp of house five and Pisces on the cusp of house eight.

The native met, fell in love, and married a person from a foreign country. The marriage partner is intellectual, attractive attractive, cultured, jovial, sympathetic, and very beneficial to the native's career. Jupiter rules house eight which strongly suggests the marriage partner is financially secure.

Chart 5: House Ruled by Planet in Aspect

The chart used here (and on pages 70 and 71) is that of a client. It is an interesting study in partnerships and financial success as the antive had two business partnerships, one domestic and one in another country. The native met his marriage partner whle in another country on business.

Empty House Judgment

There are no "empty" houses because each house has influence in a person's life. Careful observation will show how important these houses are and how active they can be. Morin established a precise method for analyzing these houses:

1. Look to the ruler of the sign on the cusp of the house in question.

2. Locate the sign the ruler is in, the house where it is posited, and its aspects.

3. Determine if the meanings of the houses can be combined by analogy.

4. Determine if the ruler permits this combination.

5. Wherever a planet is posited, the influence comes from the house it rules by sign. The house the planet rules is the cause or origin of the matter, and the house position of the planet is the effect. (See Section II on cause and effect.)

Evaluation of an Empty House

Venus, ruler of Taurus on the cusp of house six is posited in house nine in the sign of Virgo. The meanings can be combined by analogy: illness and travel. Venus, the ruler, permits this combination. Venus is a benefic, but in Virgo and ruling the malefic sixth, Venus acquires an analogy with illness. Venus is posited in house nine and rules house eleven of friends. Venus is in its fall.

Evaluation: The native would travel to see his friends due to his work (house six). The native would travel due to his health. The native's criticism of his friends could cause conflict and this would contribute to some of his nervous illnesses.

A sign always depends on the nature of its ruler and will mold itself to the nature of the planet that rules it. The influence this planet has on the sign not only lies in its essential nature but on its debility or dignity and other determinations.

Futhermore, a sign ruling a house indicates the same things as if the planet was physically present there, except to a lesser degree. But the sign will always operate by and according to the quality of its ruler. It is impor-

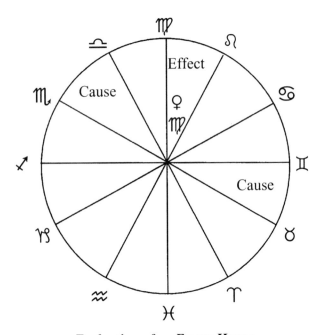

Evaluation of an Empty House

tant to remember that the physical position of a planet is the most powerful of the determing factors, and the next is rulership and then aspects.

The house meanings represent what could happen in the life of the native, and the planets materialize those people and events in a good or bad sense according to all of the determinations.

A sign on a house cusp whose ruler is absent will always act by virtue of the nature (benefic or malefic) and cosmic state of its ruler.

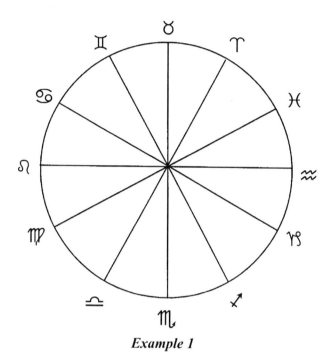

Example 1

Mundane Chart and Analogy

Another way the signs will act is by using the mundane chart. The signs of the mundane chart will bring analogy with the houses.

Example 1

Leo on the cusp of the Ascendant brings fifth house influences in the first house

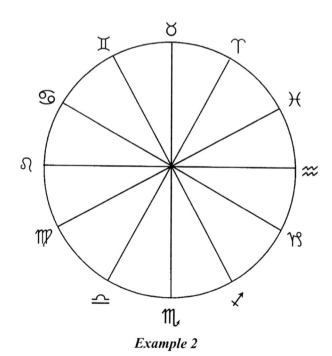

Example 2

Example 2

Libra on the cusp of house three will cause relationships to be based on mental activities.

Example 3

Virgo on the cusp of house nine brings long-distance travels related to health and work.

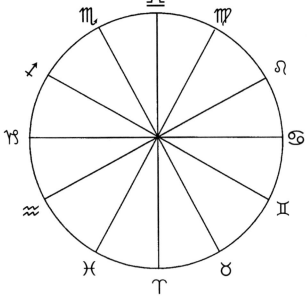

Example 3

Example 4

Taurus on the cusp of house six causes financial status to influence health and work.

Example 4

Example 5

Virgo on the cusp of house five denotes that health and employees have an influence in affairs of the heart.

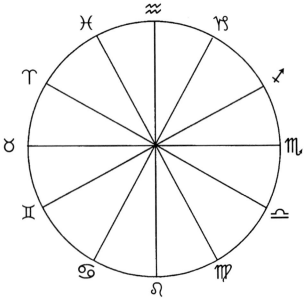

Example 5

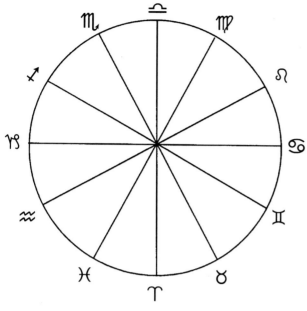

Example 6

Example 6

Gemini on the cusp of house six brings a lot of short trips and paperwork involving work or health.

Example 7

Leo is on the cusp of house twelve, indicating sorrow involving children or love affairs. This is especially dangerous if the Sun, ruler of house twelve, is in any way adversely connected with the ruler of house five, and even more so if that ruler is a malefic.

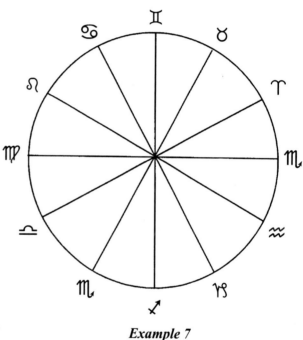

Example 7

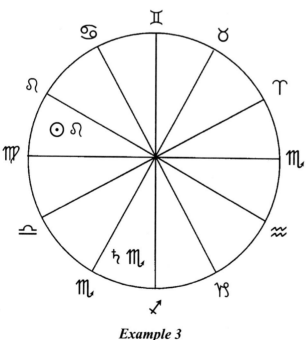

Example 3

Example 8

Leo is on the cusp of house twelve, and the Sun is posited in house twelve. Capricorn rules house five of children, and Saturn, ruler of house five, is posited in house three. The Sun and Saturn are in square aspect. House twelve is the eighth house from the fifth (the child's death). Two of the native's children had an early sudden death.

Affairs Signified by the Houses

Each house is related with determined affairs, events, and conditions in the life of the native. The house rules a determined sphere of meanings. Likewise, to each house corresponds an essential, an accidental, and a derived meaning.

1. The essential meaning is the basic concept of the house and its sphere of meanings.

2. The accidental meaning comes from the essential meaning of the opposite house. Accidentally, each house participates in the essential meanings of its opposite house. Accidentally, house two participates in "death," which is the basic concept of house eight. House eleven participates in the meanings of house five (love, children, etc.).

3. The derived significance. Any house can be the starting point depending on what is being judged (a circle without a fixed starting point). If it happens to be children, then house five would become the starting point. Children's fame, honor, success and position in life would be the tenth from the fifth, or the native's second house.

Example 1, Accidental Meaning
Mars, ruler of house two of money, is posited in house eight in Taurus. Mars is conjunct Jupiter in Taurus. Mars and Jupiter, by virtue of the opposition to house two, acquire an accidental meaning of the opposite house. After many losses (Mars in its detriment in Taurus), the native became a millionaire (Venus in its domicile in Taurus).

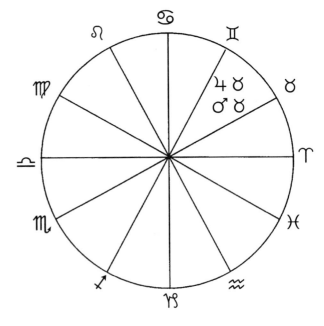

Example 1

Example 2, Derived Meaning

Some very interesting conclusions and judgments can be made with derived houses.

Jupiter, co-ruler of house seven, is posited in house four in domicile. The native's partner holds a high position in government, has achieved many awards and honors, and is well known throughout the country.

The native's fourth house is the partner's tenth house.

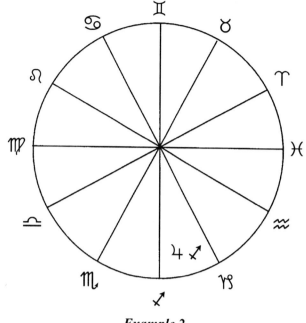

Example 2

Example 3, Essential Meaning

Morin states: ". . . in my nativity, Jupiter is in its domicile, and Venus in its exaltation, in house twelve. This has allowed me to escape from many dangerous illnesses and persecutions, which threatened me also with arrest and prison. Thanks to these positions I was also able to extract myself from the claws of my secret enemies, among which were found people of high office indicated by the Sun in house twelve and who, despite their will and power, were not able to cause me much harm."

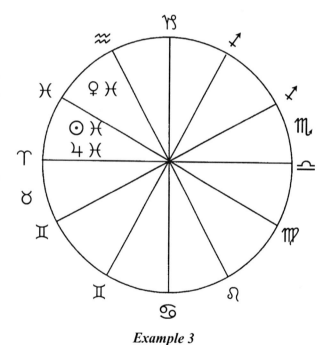

Example 3

Determination of the Effect of a Planet in a House

Sun in Aries in House Nine

Evaluation of the department of life will show how the Sun will act.

Sun in Aries in House Nine: The Sun is a benefic planet and house nine is benefic. The Sun is exalted in Aries, which will increase the strength of its effect. The Sun is in Aries, and therefore acquires analogy with house nine by being in the same triplicity.

Possible Combinations: Combination by analogy: house one and house nine, as the Sun, ruler of the Ascendent is in the ninth, a mental house. House one is also a mental house.

Theory of Determination: The department of life in which the Sun will act. The Sun will act first in the house position of the planet—traveling, foreign countries, mentality, law, science, religion, teaching, philosophy.

House of Rulership: the first house (Ascendant). The department of life would be the personality, mentality, types of persons he will come in contact with, his breadth of outlook, and health.

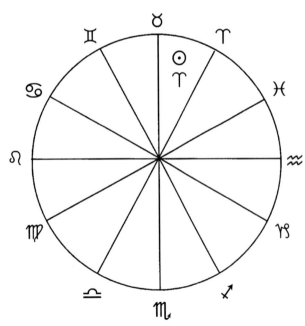

Sun in Aries in House Nine

Evaluation of the effect of the planet:

1. Quantity: a broad, brilliant mind.
2. Intensity: bold and fearless.
3. Period of life would be early.
4. Duration would be throughout life.

Pattern of the Effect of Sun in Aries, Ruler of the Ascendant, in House Nine: Character, personality, disposition: The native has an aggressive, firm, and self reliant mind. He has organizational ability and is energetic, pioneering, and an inspiration to others. Zealous and a lover of adventure, he leads an exciting and thrilling life. Noble and masterful, he is a leader of men. He has a love of power, yet he has traits of generosity combined with a resourceful nature. He has great vitality, a good physique, and a strong body and is generally very healthy. Passionate and sensual yet very dignified, his disposition is impulsive, proud, commanding. With more of a desire to lead than serve, he is argumentive, quick-tempered, self-confident, demanding, and a leader.

Travel and Foreign Countries (House Nine):

1. Quantity: the native will travel extensively in many foreign countries.
2. Intensity: the native will be extremely interested in foreign affairs, politics, law, religion.
3. Period of life would be from an early age.
4. Duration would be throughout life.

The native will have success through foreign affairs and travel, and will gain through law, science, and studies. He native will rise to a very high position of responsibility and have much success in life—a respected person, one in authority and extremely powerful. This will start very early in life and last throughout life.

This example is from the chart of William I, the first emperor of Germany and a very capable general. He declared war against Denmark, Austria, and France to unite all Germans under one empire, and he and Bismarck were the unifiers of Germany. He became an officer at age ten, colonel at age twenty, and major general at age twenty-one. William I lived until he was ninety-one—an example of Leo ascending with the Sun in Aries in exaltation and in good cosmic state and posited in house nine.

Theory of Determination: Determination relates to the house in which planetary activity takes place. In order of strength, a planet acts:

1. In the house in which it is located; here, it has the most influence.
2. In the house it rules, and sometimes through exalted rulership.
3. In the house to which it sends an aspect.
4. In the house where its dispositor is placed.
5. In the house ruled by a planet in aspect.

Evaluation of the Effect of a Planet in a House

Following is the determination of the department of life in which Venus will act and the possible combinations.

Venus in Pisces in House Seven:

1. Will act first in the house position of the planet, which is house seven of partnerships, marriage, open enemies.

2. Will act next in the house of rulership. Venus rules Libra on the cusp of house two of money, possessions and financial endeavors.

3. Venus rules Taurus on the cusp of house nine of travel, foreign affairs, law, politics, publications, religion, and the mentality.

Possible Combinations:

1. House seven is marriage and house two is money. Gain of money through marriage.

2. House seven is the partner and house nine is travel. The native will accompany the partner in travel to foreign countries. The partner has a love of philosophy, religion, writing, law, politics, foreign affairs.

3. Houses two and nine indicate the partner may gain money through travel to a foreign country, and through writing.

4. Houses seven, two, and nine indicate the partner may gain money through publishing of music, poetry, drama or art.

Evaluation of the Effect of Venus in House Seven:

1. Quantity: More than one marriage; may have a secret love.

2. Intensity: Love will be very deep in one of the relationships.

3. Period of life would be early.

4. Duration would be long lasting.

5. Possibility of *transformation* of planetary action—yes, but see below under open enemies.

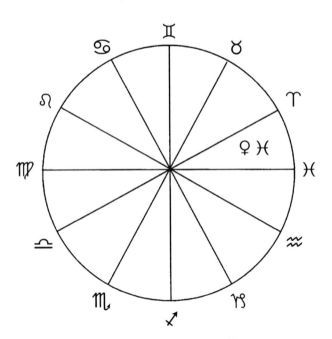

Venus in Pisces in House Seven

80

Pattern of the Effects of Venus in House Seven:

The marriage or partnership will be a very happy one. The partner will be attractive, compassionate, romantic, and affectionate. As a lover of beauty there will be much interest in poetry, drama, music, and art. The marriage or partnership will be one of great sacrifice and love. (This example is from the nativity of Juliet Drouse, mistress of Victor Hugo. She traveled with him and accompanied him in his exile.)

The reasons for the above are:

1. *Essential nature*: Venus is a benefic planet in a benefic house.
2. *Natural analogy*: Venus has analogy with house seven, and therefore with love and marriage.
3. *Cosmic state*: Venus is exalted in Pisces.

House seven is partially benefic (marriage) and partially malefic (open enemies). Continuing the reading of Venus in house seven, it is unlikely the native will have angry confrontations or open enemies because Venus is exalted in Pisces. If angry confrontations from an enemy come to the native, that person will eventually become a friend. Or the confrontation will benefit the native in a noticeable way. This is called *transformation*.

Transformation occurs when a benefic planet in good cosmic state is in a malefic house. The planet has no analogy with the house; therefore, transformation can occur. Or it can occur when a malefic planet is in a bad cosmic state in a benefic house. These are the only two combinations where conditions can actually transform.

Summary of the Steps in the Evaluation of the Effect of a Planet in a House

1. Is the essential nature of the planet benefic or malefic?

2. Is the house benefic or malefic?

3. Does the planet's essential nature have analogy with the house through sign or aspect?

4. Does the planet acquire analogy with the house?

5. What is the cosmic state of the planet . . . debility, dignity, triplicity, or peregrine?

6. Determine in what department of life the planet will act: house position, and house of rulership (may combine the house of position with house of rulership when there is analogy).

7. Determine by position (or rulership) the planet's capacity to produce:

   Quantity: no money or great wealth; few, no, or many children and many or few friends

   Intensity: abrupt, bitter, slight, forceful, dangerous, fantastic, etc.

   Speed of realization: childhood, teenage, mid life, late life

   Duration: length of time; for example, six months, thirty years, forever, etc.

   Possibility of transformation

   Pattern of the effects of a particular planet in the house.

Always remember: the cosmic state of the planet and analogy are the keys.

The House of Life

The first house signifies the native and all the events and matters that affect his body, soul, mind, and spirit. Morin attributes to this house the life, general state of health, predisposition for determined illnesses, the temperament, and moral and intellectual inclinations. He emphasizes the importance of any aspects to the ascending degree and considers them as more important and potent than those to the ruler of house one.

The house where the ruler of the Ascendant is posited will be very important in the native's life. The native will have a desire for the people and things represented by this house, and he will be subject to the influences of these people and matters and can gain or suffer from them.

A planet located in the first house will have a great influence on the character, temperament, and disposition of the native. Any planet conjunct the Ascendant or the ruler of house one will give a discription of the types of persons with whom the native will come in contact.

General Rules to Determine the Character, Personality, and Temperament

1. If the ruler of house one is found in another house, or if the ruler of another house is found in house one, the meanings of these houses often combine and the matters signified will materialize.

2. Determine if the planet in a house has analogy or is antagonistic.

3. Character and mentality can be judged only by the first, third, and ninth houses and planets therein, the planets ruling these houses, and the aspects. Any planet that is not involved in these three houses is not related to the native's character or mentality.

4. Give particular importance to the essential nature and cosmic state of the ruler of the Ascendant and if it is favorable or unfavorable.

5. If the ruler of the Ascendant or a planet in house one is in domicile, it will bestow great benefits and satisfaction in many areas of life according to the meanings of the planet, houses, and sign involved. These will be constant and ongoing because of the superior cosmic state of the planet.

6. If the ruler of the Ascendant is in exaltation, the native can expect rewards for hard work and good things will come in life through a combination of luck and hard work. These will be obtained with some difficulty and will come intermittently. However, the native will always thrive.

7. If the ruler of the Ascendant is in triplicity, the native will receive advantages through the advice and intervention of others.

Example 1

The ruler of house one is in house ten. The native pursues success, and much of his energy is used in the pursuit of a successful career. He needs recognition and is driven by his personal initiative and ambition. Cause: first house (native). Effect: tenth house success. The native seeks success.

Example 2

The ruler of house ten is in house one. Success and honors come to the native without too much effort on his part. Cause: house ten (honors and success). Effect: house one (native). Success comes to the native without much effort on his part.

House one signifies the native. The other houses and their meanings signify matters that may befall the native. If the ruler of the Ascendant is in detriment or fall and conjunct, square, or opposition a malefic, it will exert an unfavorable influence on the things signifed by the Ascendant.

If the planet ruling the Ascendant is not in domicile, exaltation, fall, or detriment, it depends on the nature and cosmic state of its disposer. Morin calls this the "secondary ruler" and gives it a dominant role in synthesis.

Any planet in house one has a great influence on the temperament, character, and disposition. These influences are usually obvious and act continuously throughout life.

Any planet connected with the ruler of house one will have a strong influence on matters of house one.

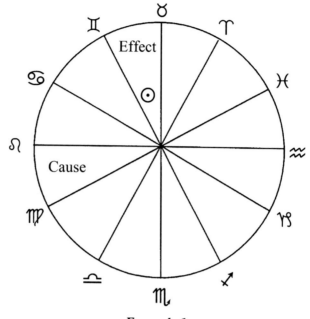

Example 1

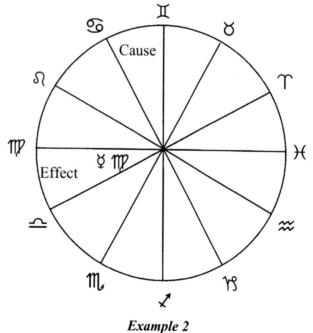

Example 2

Morin considers it worse for the ascending degree to be afflicted by a square or an opposition from Mars or Saturn than for the ruler of the Ascendant to be afflicted by these malefics. (The birth time must be accurate in order to use aspects to the ascending degree.)

Judge each planet ruling the Ascendant by its nature, its sign, its dispositor, its house, and its aspects. Do the same for each planet in house one. All will have an effect on the character, personality, and moral and intellectual inclinations. Then give special attention to aspects to the ascending degree.

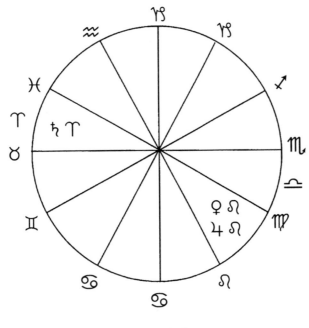

Example 3

Example 3

When the ruler of house one is in another house, the meanings of both houses usually combine and the matters are important to the native. Venus, ruler of the Ascendant, is in Leo in house five. The client was interested in her love life. Venus is conjunct Jupiter; therefore, the love affairs did materialize. However, this conjunction is trine to Saturn in Aries (its fall) in house twelve. Venus and Jupiter in Leo in house five has analogy with love affairs. Saturn in Aries has analogy with sadness and heartache. This is an example of planets with opposite meanings, and houses that are opposite in nature, connecting with each other.

The client was attractive and had a loving, radiant personality. She said her love affairs brought her sadness and solitude, In this example, Venus, Saturn, and Jupiter involve houses one, five, six, eight, and twelve.

The House of Death

The meaning of the eighth house—death (the native's death)—can only be caused through the affairs of some other house. Many times this is in the form of a sudden death caused by others, either directly or indirectly. Accidents can cut life short, and frequently do so.

Except in the case of sudden death by accident, philosophically we all die "daily." Many of the reasons are not so obvious: greed, anger, hate, fear, revenge, guilt, self-indulgence, and self-gratification, just to mention a few.

Granted, no astrologer should predict death. Nor can we let anyone move blindly into danger or disaster, such as surgery, travel, or major decisions at the wrong time, involvements with dangerous associates, danger from drugs, or any exciting adventure that indicates a threat to life. The list goes on and on.

It is true that the astrologer should never alarm. If any danger is observed in the chart, counsel in as constructive and positive manner as possible. Forewarned is forearmed, and by knowing, one may take special precautions and perhaps prevent the adversity.

Since everyone is the master of his or her own destiny, there is no rule to judge another with finality.

To make a judgment, observe the nature of the planet in question, its essential nature, the sign it is in, and its cosmic state. If the planet is not in domicile (its own sign), the dispositor should be carefully analyzed. The ruler of the Ascendant (or rulers) should be judged in the same manner, as this is the house of life, the temperament and disposition, attitudes, conduct, and moral and intellectual inclinations.

When a planet in house eight rules two other houses, determine which meanings can most effectively combine. Of the two houses, the one which the planet most closely cooperates with will usually bring a threat to life.

The ruler of house eight in house one, or the ruler of house one in house eight, can be an indication of a premature death usually caused by the native himself. This could be by exposing himself to danger, voluntarily or unconsciously.

The ruler of any house in house eight is an indication that death could be caused by the person or affairs signified by the house it rules. (Mercury in house eight rules house three, which indicates an auto accident.)

The ruler of house eight in another house is an indication of an indirect cause of death.

Attention must be paid to any planet that the ruler of house eight is conjunct, especially if it is conjunct Mars.

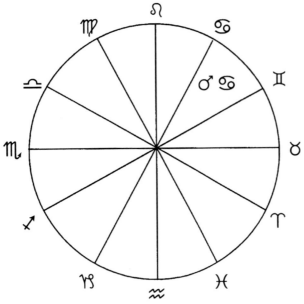

Example 1

Examples 1 and 2

This is an indication of a premature death caused by the native by exposing himself to danger, or by trying to escape death by taking precautions—such as surgery at the wrong time. But all the factors must be examined, especially all the determinations of Mars and Mercury.

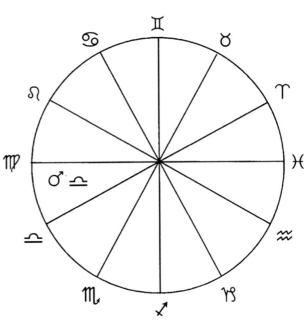

Example 2

Example 3

The ruler of house seven in house eight indicates the spouse, an enemy, or war or fights could cause the native's death.

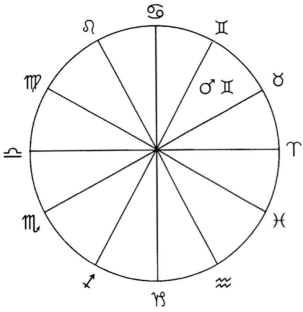

Example 3

Example 4

The ruler of house eleven in house eight indicates a friend could bring about the native's death.

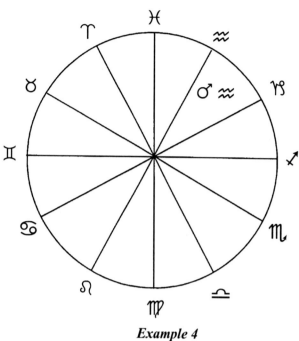

Example 4

The ruler of house twelve in house eight indicates illness or a secret enemy, or poor care while confined in the hospital causes death.

Example 5

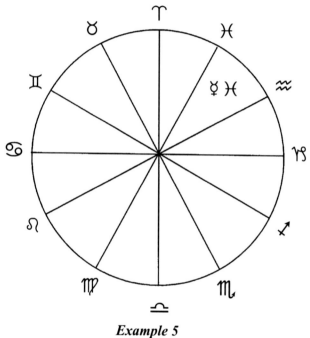

Example 5

Example 6

The ruler of houses two and seven in house eight indicates that greed, theives, or robbers could cause death.

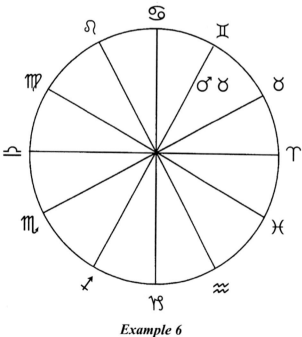

Example 6

87

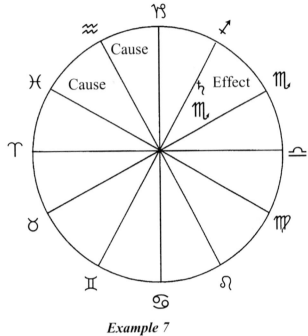

Example 7

Example 7

The ruler of houses ten and eleven in house eight indicates an acquaintance through business is with the native at death or causes the native's death.

Example 8

The ruler of houses one and six in house eight indicates illness causes death.

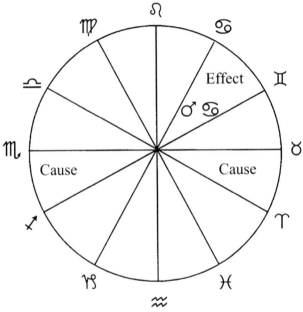

Example 8

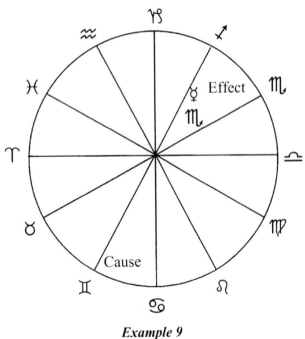

Example 9

Example 9

The ruler of house three in house eight indicates that a car accident or neighbors could cause death.

Example 10

The ruler of house nine in house eight indicates the native was involved with foreigners or distant travel at the time of death.

Always consider the analogy the planet has with the house in question. And as stated earlier, all the determinations must be carefully examined.

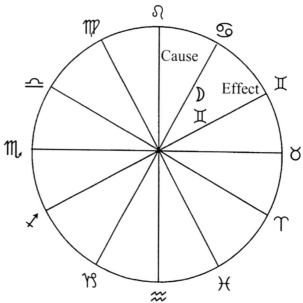

Example 10

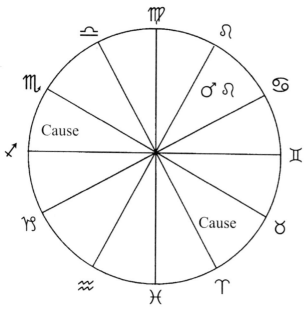

Example 11

Example 11

The ruler of houses five and twelve in house eight indicates a lover, childbirth, or disease from pleasures could cause the native's death.

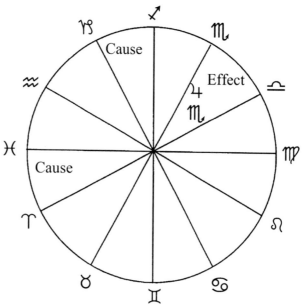

Example 12

The ruler of houses one and ten in house eight indicates a public death sentence.

Example 12

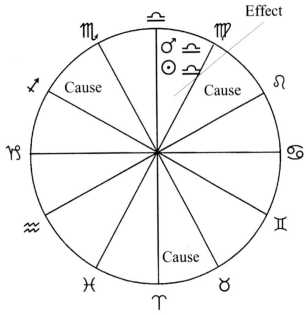

Example 13

Example 13

A serious auto accident while traveling with a friend brought a brush with death. Always note the cosmic state of a planet, and consider the houses the planet rules while looking for any analogies that exist between them. If there is a conjunction and one of the planets rules house eight, carefully note the houses each rules and combine them by analogy.

Example 14

The ruler of house twelve and house eight are conjunct in house six indicates that an illness that confines the native will be dangerous to his or her life.

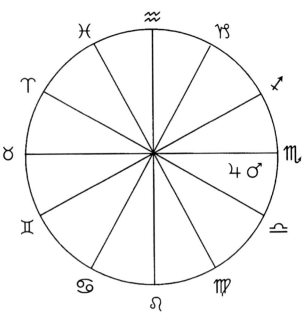

Example 14

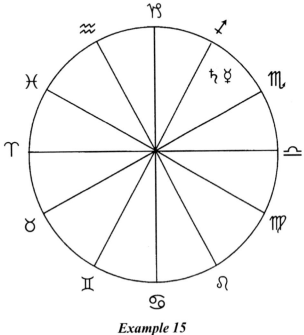

Example 15

Example 15

The ruler of house eleven is conjunct the ruler of house three in house eight. A friend could cause the native's death while on a short trip with an auto accident as a possible cause.

Example 16

The ruler of houses two and seven is in house eight conjunct the ruler of houses twelve and nine. An open or secret enemy, travel, politics, foreigners, or money, could cause the native's death. The enemies have the strongest analogies. (This configuration is from the chart of John F. Kennedy. Capricorn is on the cusp of house four, the end of life. The ruler, Saturn, is in house ten. Death came while involved in professional matters.) Saturn is in exile in house ten, which indicates great success followed by downfall.

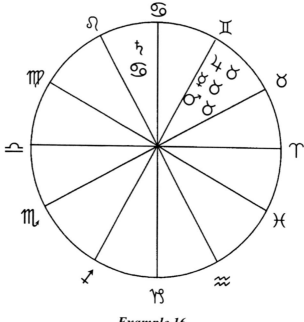

Example 16

Example 17

This indicates violent death through one's own actions. In this case the ruler of houses one and ten is in house eight, Jupiter is in Scorpio, and Jupiter in house eight is disposed by Mars in house nine. The native received a death sentence from a jury when he was found guilty of murder. (From the chart of Bruno Richart Hauptman, kidnapper of the Lindbergh baby.)

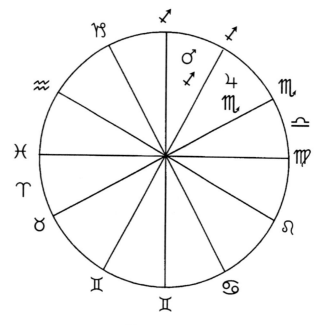

Example 17

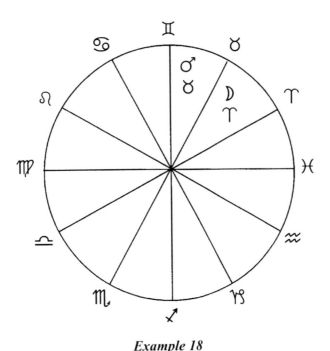

Example 18

Example 18

Violent death caused by the native's beliefs. Mars, ruler of houses three and eight, is in house nine. The Moon, ruler of house eleven, is in house eight and its dispositor is Mars; Mars is in its detriment. The native's beliefs, friends, foreign affairs, and travel all related to his death. (From the chart of Pierre Laval, French Statesman.) He was accused of treason and sentenced to death. He was shot by a firing squad.

When many planets are in the house, the most powerful action will come from the one which is also the house ruler; next, the one possessing closest natural analogy with the house meanings; and last, the planet closest to the house cusp. If many planets are in the house and their dispositor is in another, the affairs indicated by this dispositor will form the point of departure for whatever the group of planets produces. Yet each planet will work independently.

Example 19

Mars, ruler of houses three and eight, is posited in house two. By virtue of the opposition to house eight, Mars acquires an accidental meaning of the opposite house. Mars has analogy with death. If all the other determinations are adverse, there is danger to the native's life. Mars is in detriment, square both the Sun and Moon. Mars is disposed by Venus in Virgo in house twelve. Venus is in fall. Venus rules houses two and nine.

The native met an early and violent death while walking to the neighborhood store. He was attacked, robbed, and murdered by transients.

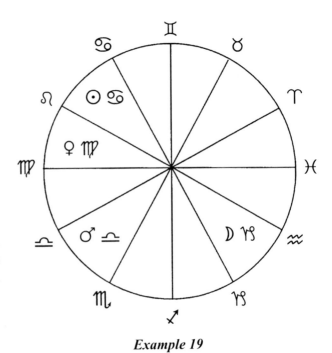

Example 19

Important Points to Remember

- Clearly formulated rules provide a foundation to reading a chart.
- The examples set forth in this book should not be taken as a formula of fixed application because the entire chart is not shown.
- Illustrations such as "planet A in house B" purposely focus on only a few essential factors of a whole series.
- All of the example charts used in this book are those of former clients.
- Remember to use:
    - Planets in relationship to the house (see page 25): transformation, analogy, cosmic state, and malefic vs. benefic planets are the basics to accurate chart reading.
    - Cause and effect, which is used liberally throughout this book, is a starting point to discuss a particular event shown in a chart. Effect is the planet's placement, and cause is the cusp ruled by that planet.
    - Natural analogy is when the planet and house meanings agree.
    - Acquired anaology is when the sign the planet is in agrees with the house meanings, or an aspect agrees with the house meanings.
    - Cosmic state (the sign a planet is in): whether a planet is in domicile, exaltation, fall, detriment (also called exile), triplicity, or preregrine.
    - Use dispositors.

With a basic knowledge of astrology and employing the above, you will become a devoted fan of Morin. These are the basic building blocks of a solid understanding of how to begin to read a chart.

Never forget the divine gift of free will. The way in which people apply their individual gifts is in their own hands.

Major Points to Consider When Making a Determination

When judging the cosmic state of a planet it should also be taken into consideration if the planet is:

1. Oriental or occidental of the Sun. A planet is oriental of the Sun if it rises after the Sun.

2. If the planet is fast, there is more probability of a speedy realization of the effects toward which it is determined. If the planet is slow, the effects could be delayed. If the planet is retrograde, the effects could be hindered, and there is an interruption or incomplete results of the matters indicated. Direct movement brings progress of the planetary effect, while a stationary planet indicates some stability and endurance of its effects.

3. Consider the kind of house occupied: angular, succedent, or cadent. When a planet falls into an angular house, its effect will increase.

4. A solitary planet (not connected to any other planet by aspect or conjunction) indicates something unusual concerning the affairs of the house it occupies.

5. A judgment should never be made on any particular house or matter before considering the planets in that house, the ruler of the house, the planet that rules this ruler, and if these planets are related to each other.

6. When two planets are conjunct, a determination must be made. Does either planet have analogy with the house? Are both planets in "acceptable" cosmic state? If so, these planets become partners, with each adding its own infleunce, and together they realize the goal of the promises of the house. If they are both in bad cosmic state, they will work against the meaning of the house. If there is one of each, then they are judged independently. Examples: Jupiter conjunct Saturn in Taurus indicates an opportunity to make money (Jupiter) and keep money (Saturn). Mars conjunct Venus in Libra indictes intelligent, beautiful partners, but also constant bickering and stressful arguments that can ruin the relationship. Saturn conjunct Mercury in Capricorn indicates a deep, penetrating mind, such as that of a scientist, computer programmer, researcher, etc.

7. One can usually judge from the beginning if the horoscope is fortunate or unfortunate by properly evaluating planets in houses one and ten. Also look at the lights (Sun and Moon) to determine if one or the other is afflicted.

The Power of the Aspects

Aspects constitute an essential factor of the determinations. Some of the basic rules are listed below:

1. The planet's nature (benefic or malefic).

2. The sign in which the planet is posited (benefic or malefic).

3. If the planet is in exaltation, domicile, fall, detriment, triplicity or peregrine.

4. The house in which the planet is posited (malefic or benefic).

5. The houses the planets in question rule .

6. The nature of the aspect (trine, square, etc.).

7. The sign where the aspect falls and the planet ruling that sign.

8. The house or houses.

9. The circumstances before and after the aspect.

10. Analogy between planet and house and the planet's cosmic state are key.

- A benefic planet, in bad cosmic state, receiving good aspects, will produce only small advantages. Receiving bad aspects, some problems or much damage (depending on the planet sending the bad aspect; that is, if the planet is benefic or malefic).

- A malefic planet in bad cosmic state receiving bad aspects will cause serious problems in the affairs of the house in which they fall. The harmful effects of its essential malefic nature are magnified.

- Good aspects from a benefic planet produce positive effects with ease and abundance. They bring the good things indicated by the houses where they fall and prevent problems from happening.

- A malefic planet receiving good aspects will produce a certain amount of success and benefits in the middle of difficulties.

- To evaluate the power and quality of the effects produced by a given aspect, it is important to consider the house and if it is angular. All things being equal, when an aspect falls into an angular house, the effect will increase.

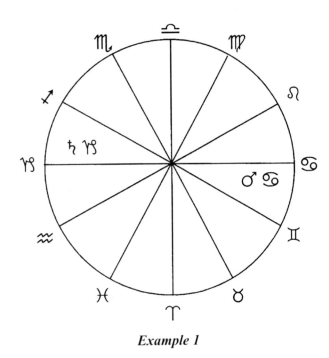

Example 1

Example 1

The cosmic state of the planet in question should be considered, along with its essential nature and house position.

1. Saturn in Capricorn in house twelve.

2. Saturn in Capricorn is in domicile.

3. Saturn is a malefic planet.

4. Saturn in house twelve receives an opposition from Mars in Cancer.

5. Mars in Cancer is a malefic in fall. The sixth house is a malefic house.

Therefore, Saturn will gain an extreme power for evil since by its nature it tends more to evil than good. Two malefics in malefic houses have analogy with the matters (illness) of houses six and twelve.

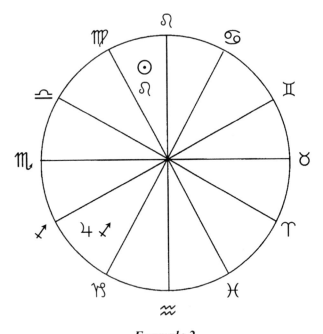

Example 2

Example 2

Sun is in Leo in house ten in domicile receiving a trine from Jupiter in Sagittarius in house two in domicile.

1. Honors, dignities, success, fame, and prestige, which will be realized with certainty and bringing an abundance of wealth and good fortune. This will start early in life and last throughout life. Both benefics are in benefic houses in domicile, and have analogy with the planets' signs and houses.

Section IV

Example Charts for Study

The following notable nativities have been included for the purpose of practice work. Many of the configurations have been included in the examples throughout this book, while other examples are from my client files. The information on death included various configurations from the many horoscopes collected through the years for research on sudden death (by accident, murder and suicide).

In the following examples it is best to proceed by first determining the specific matter, circumstance, event, or quality to be evaluated, which is indicated with each chart.

As a guide in this practice work , each chart is numbered and the department of life to be evaluated is listed by number. Based on the material learned and by following Morin's systematic approach, the value and meaning of his teachings should add a new dimension to the interpretation of the natal figure that will eventually lead to superior astrological synthesis.

Example 1, Billy Carter

Evalute: brothers and sisters.

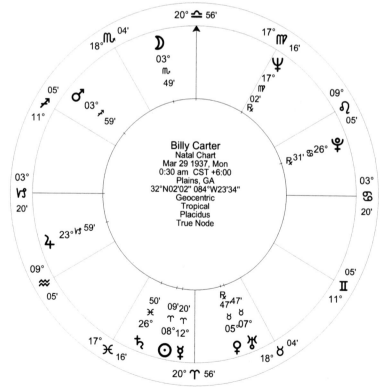

Billy Carter
Natal Chart
Mar 29 1937, Mon
0:30 am CST +6:00
Plains, GA
32°N02'02" 084°W23'34"
Geocentric
Tropical
Placidus
True Node

*Billy Carter, brother of former President Jimmy Carter;
source: Dell Horoscope.*

Example 2, Shah of Iran

Evaluate: conditions surrounding the end of life.

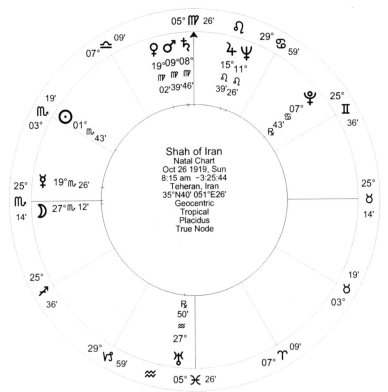

Shah of Iran; source: Ebertin.

Example 3, Montgomery Clift

Evaluate: love life.

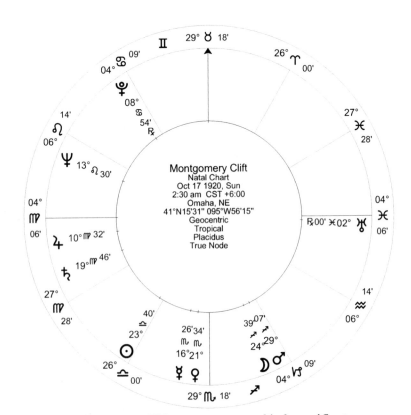

Montgomery Clift, actor; source: birth certificate.

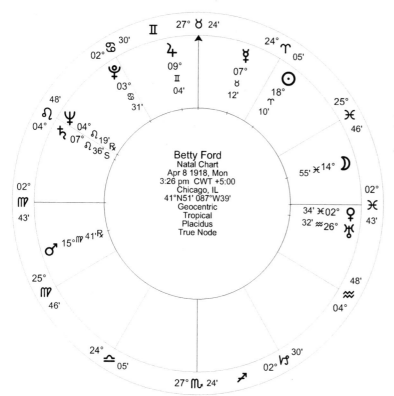

Example 4, Betty Ford

Evaluate: health.

Betty Ford, former First Lady; source: Mercury Hour.

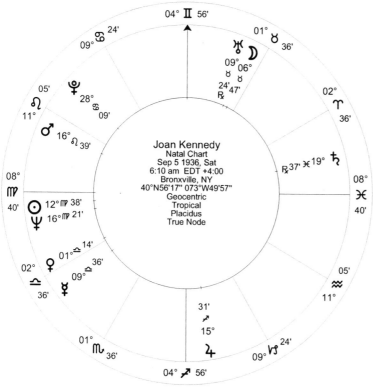

Example 5, Joan Kennedy

Evaluate: marriage partner.

*Joan Kennedy, former wife of U.S. Senator Ted Kennedy;
source: Dell Horoscope.*

Example 6, Hamilton Jordan

Evaluate: open enemies.

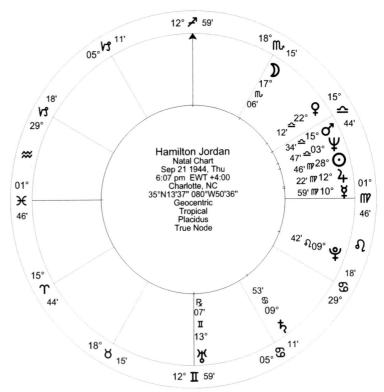

Hamilton Jordan, former chief of staff to Jimmy Carter, former U.S. president; source: Missouri Federation of Astrologers

Example 7, John F. Kennedy

Evaluate: death.

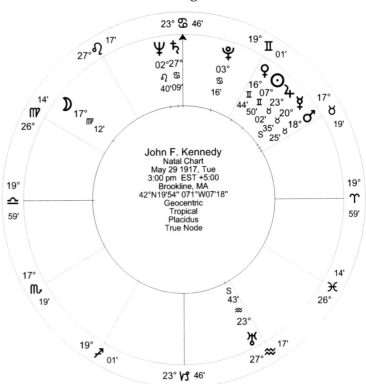

John F. Kennedy, former U.S. president, murdered; source: **Horoscopes of U.S. Presidents.**

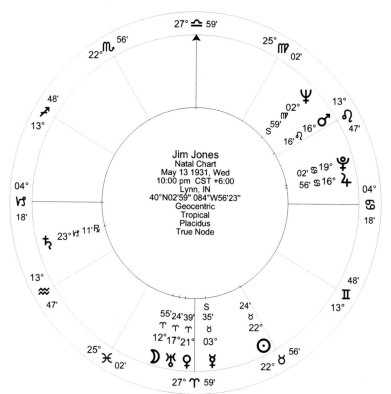

Example 8, Jim Jones

Evaluate: death.

Jim Jones, Peoples Temple Founder, death by suicide; source:
***Dell* Horoscope.**

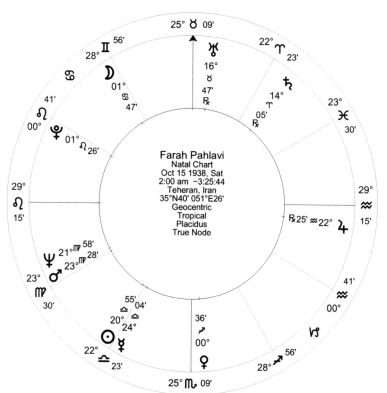

Example 9, Farah Pahlavi

Evaluate: foreign countries.

Farah Pahlavi, Empress of Iran; source: **Profiles of Women.**

Example 10, Anita Bryant

Evaluate: beliefs, religion, spirituality.

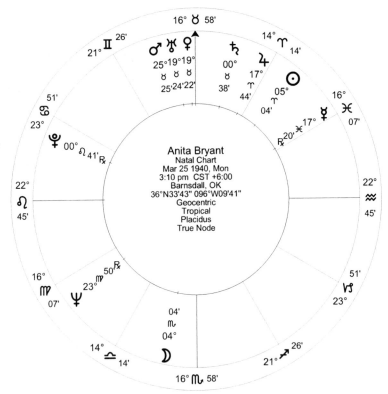

Anita Bryant, singer and gay rights opponent;
source: **Mercury Hour.**

Example 11, Robert F. Kennedy

Evaluate: fame and prestige.

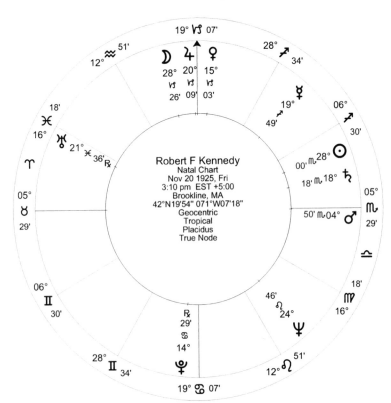

Robert F. Kennedy, former U.S. senator;
source: birth certificate.

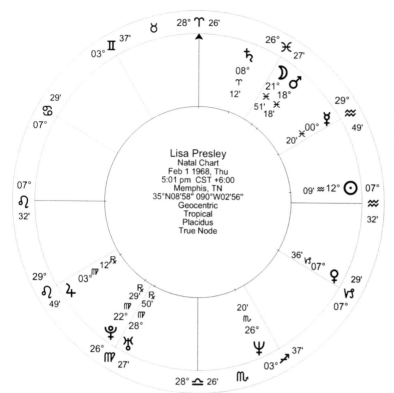

Example 12, Lisa Presley

Evaluate: parents.

Lisa Presley, daughter of singer Elvis Presley; source: birth certificate.

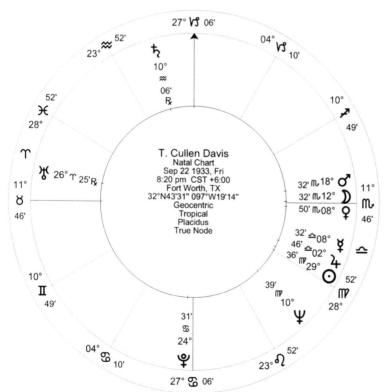

Example 13, T. Cullen Davis

Evaluate: friends.

T. Cullen Davis, millionaire; source: from Cullen to a friend.

Example 17, Morgan Marshack

Evaluate: friends.

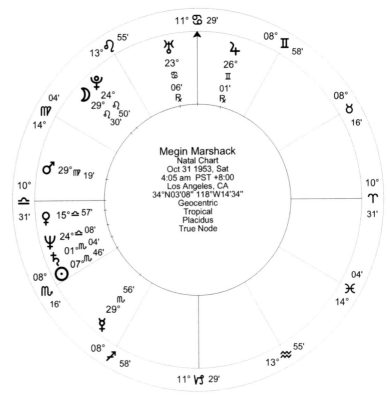

Morgan Marshack, former business associate/partner of Nelson Rockefeller; source: birth certificate.

Example 18, John Dean

Evaluate: confinement.

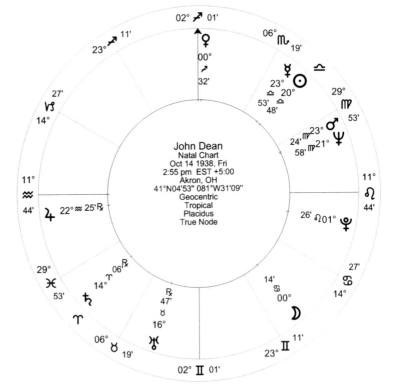

John Dean, former White House counsel to Richard Nixon, served a sentence of four months for felony convictions; source: birth certificate.

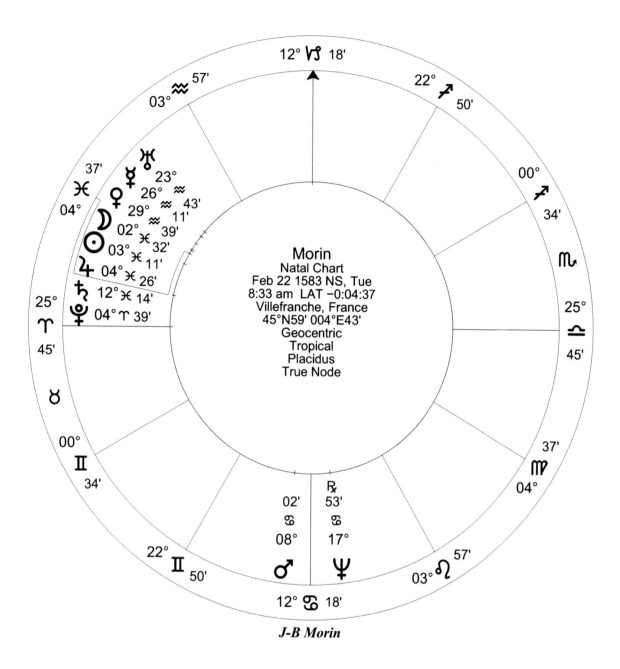

J-B Morin

Translations of the Astrologia Gallica
published by the American Federation of Astrologers

Books 13, 14, 15, & 19: The Natures of the Planets and the Fixed Stars, The Primum Caelum and Its Division into 12 Parts, The Essential Dignities of the Planets, and The Elements of Astrology or The Principles of Judgments. 2006. Translated by James H. Holden

Book 16: The Rays and Aspects of the Planets. 2008. Translated by James H. Holden

Book 17: The Astrological Houses. 2008. Translated by James H. Holden

Book 18: The Strengths of the Planets. 2004. Translated from the Spanish version of Pepita Sanchis Llacer by Anthony Louis LaBruzza

Book 21: The Morinus System of Horoscope Interpretation. 2008.
Translated by Richard S. Baldwin

Book 22: Primary Directions. 1994. Translated by James H. Holden

Book 23: Revolutions. 2002, 2003. Translated by James H. Holden

Book 24: Progressions and Transits. 2004. Translated by James H. Holden

Book 25: The Universal Constitutions of the Caelum. 2008. Translated by James H. Holden

Book 26: Astrological Interrogations and Elections. 2010. Translated by James H. Holden

Also, a book of charts:
Astrologia Gallica Horoscopes by James H. Holden (2011)

About the Author

Patti Tobin Brittain is a professional astrologer with many years of experience in the field. In addition to her private practice in Dallas, her activities have included counseling, teaching, writing, research, speaking engagements, and conducting seminars.

Patti received professional certification from the American Federation of Astrologers and is a member of that organization. She also earned certification for her professional competence from the Missouri Federation of Astrologers. Patti is a past president of the Texas Astrological Association.

Patti is well known for her predictions on the national scene and has written for numerous publications, including *Travelhost*, *Texas Woman*, and *Midnight Globe*.

CPSIA information can be obtained at www.ICGtesting.com

233847LV00002B/19/P